Strum and Drang

Strum and Drang

Great Moments in Rock 'n' Roll

by

Joel Orff

www.jorff.com

joelorff@yahoo.com

Strum and Drang Great Moments in Rock 'n' Roll is published by Alternative Comics, 503 NW 37th Ave., Gainesville, FL 32609-2204; 352.373.6336; jmason@indyworld.com; www.indyworld.com/altcomics. All contents copyright (c) 1999, 2000, 2001, 2002, 2003 Joel Orff. All rights reserved. Characters and likenesses are properties of Joel Orff. Graphic Design: Charles Orr. Publisher: Jeff Mason. No portion of this book may be reprinted or reproduced without permission except for journalistic or educational purposes. First Printing, May 2003. Printed in Canada. ISBN 1-891867-27-X

Special thanks to everyone who sent in their stories.

Many thanks to my family, Jeff Mason, Charlie Orr, Ian Rans, Jim DeRogatis, John Porcellino, Delaine Derry Green, Mark Cunningham and Jenny Zervakis, Jeff Zenick, Jennifer Contino, Alice Dubois, Lori Wray, The Autumn Leaves, Anchorhead, Richard Gatten, King Crab, Mad Dog, O'Mal, Monk, Stoke, Hinz and of course Maaac, who inspired the whole thing.

For Tony and Andi

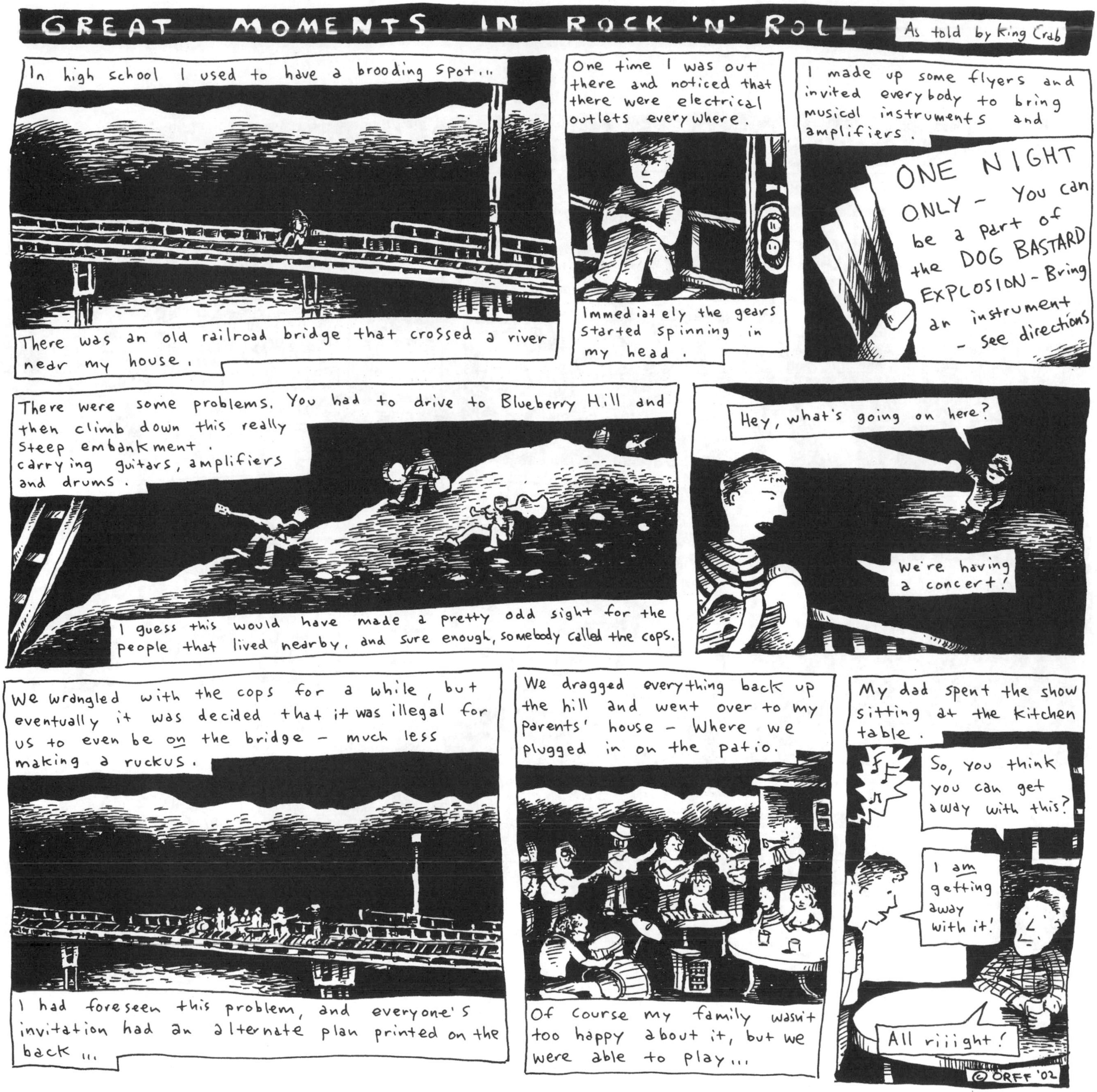
GREAT MOMENTS IN ROCK 'N' ROLL
As told by King Crab
In high school I used to have a brooding spot...
There was an old railroad bridge that crossed a river near my house.
One time I was out there and noticed that there were electrical outlets everywhere.
Immediately the gears started spinning in my head.
I made up some flyers and invited everybody to bring musical instruments and amplifiers.
ONE NIGHT ONLY - You can be a part of the DOG BASTARD EXPLOSION - Bring an instrument - see directions
There were some problems. You had to drive to Blueberry Hill and then climb down this really steep embankment. carrying guitars, amplifiers and drums.
I guess this would have made a pretty odd sight for the people that lived nearby, and sure enough, somebody called the cops.
Hey, what's going on here?
We're having a concert!
We wrangled with the cops for a while, but eventually it was decided that it was illegal for us to even be on the bridge - much less making a ruckus.
I had foreseen this problem, and everyone's invitation had an alternate plan printed on the back...
We dragged everything back up the hill and went over to my parents' house - Where we plugged in on the patio.
Of course my family wasn't too happy about it, but we were able to play...
My dad spent the show sitting at the kitchen table.
So, you think you can get away with this?
I am getting away with it!
All riiight!
© ORFF '02

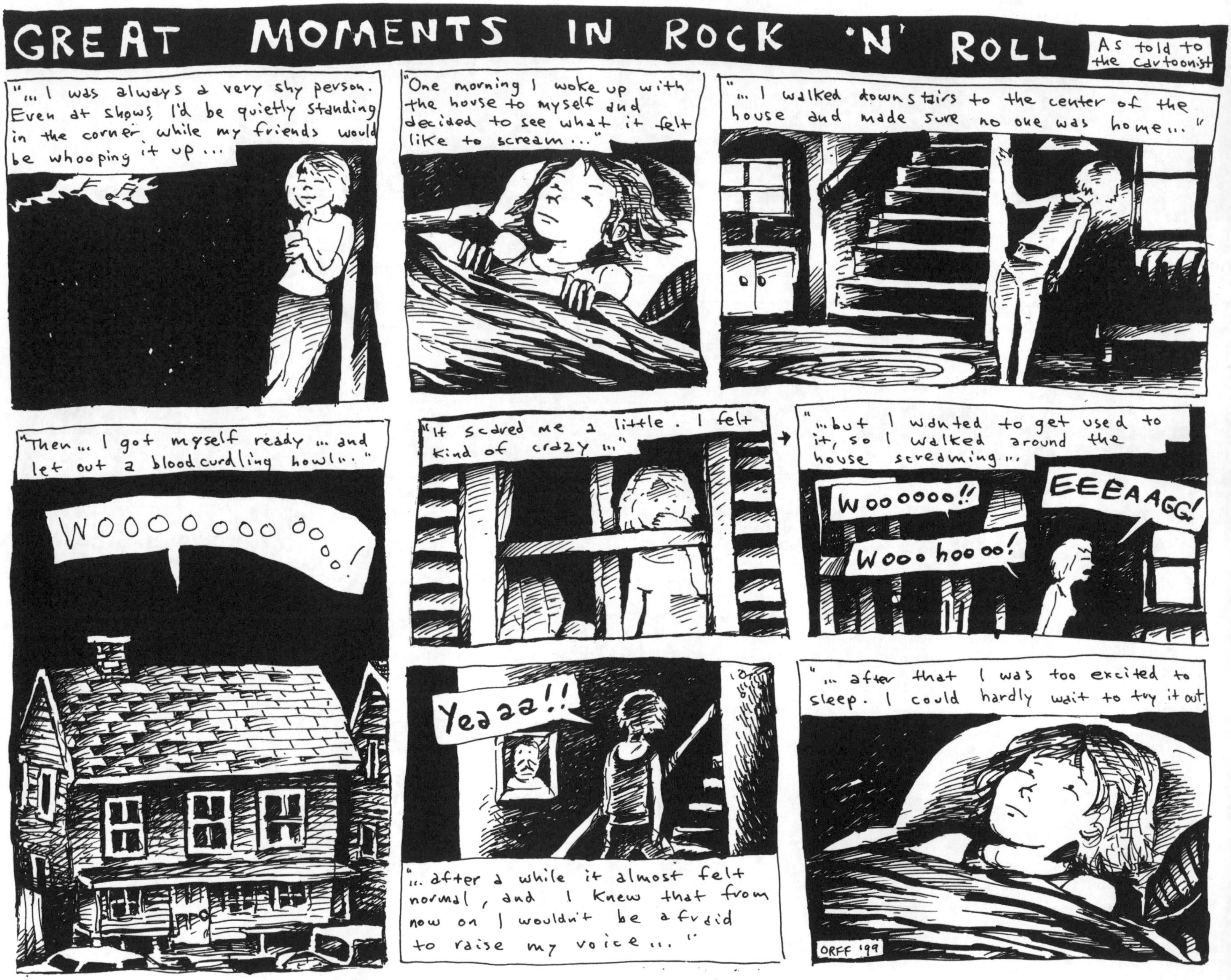
GREAT MOMENTS IN ROCK 'N' ROLL
As told to the cartoonist
"... I was always a very shy person. Even at shows, I'd be quietly standing in the corner while my friends would be whooping it up ...
"One morning I woke up with the house to myself and decided to see what it felt like to scream ..."
"... I walked downstairs to the center of the house and made sure no one was home ..."
"Then ... I got myself ready ... and let out a bloodcurdling howl ..."
WOOOOOOOOOOO!
"It scared me a little. I felt kind of crazy ..."
"... but I wanted to get used to it, so I walked around the house screaming ...
WOOOOOO!!
EEEAAGG!
Wooohoooo!
Yeaaa!!
"... after a while it almost felt normal, and I knew that from now on I wouldn't be afraid to raise my voice ..."
"... after that I was too excited to sleep. I could hardly wait to try it out.
ORFF '99

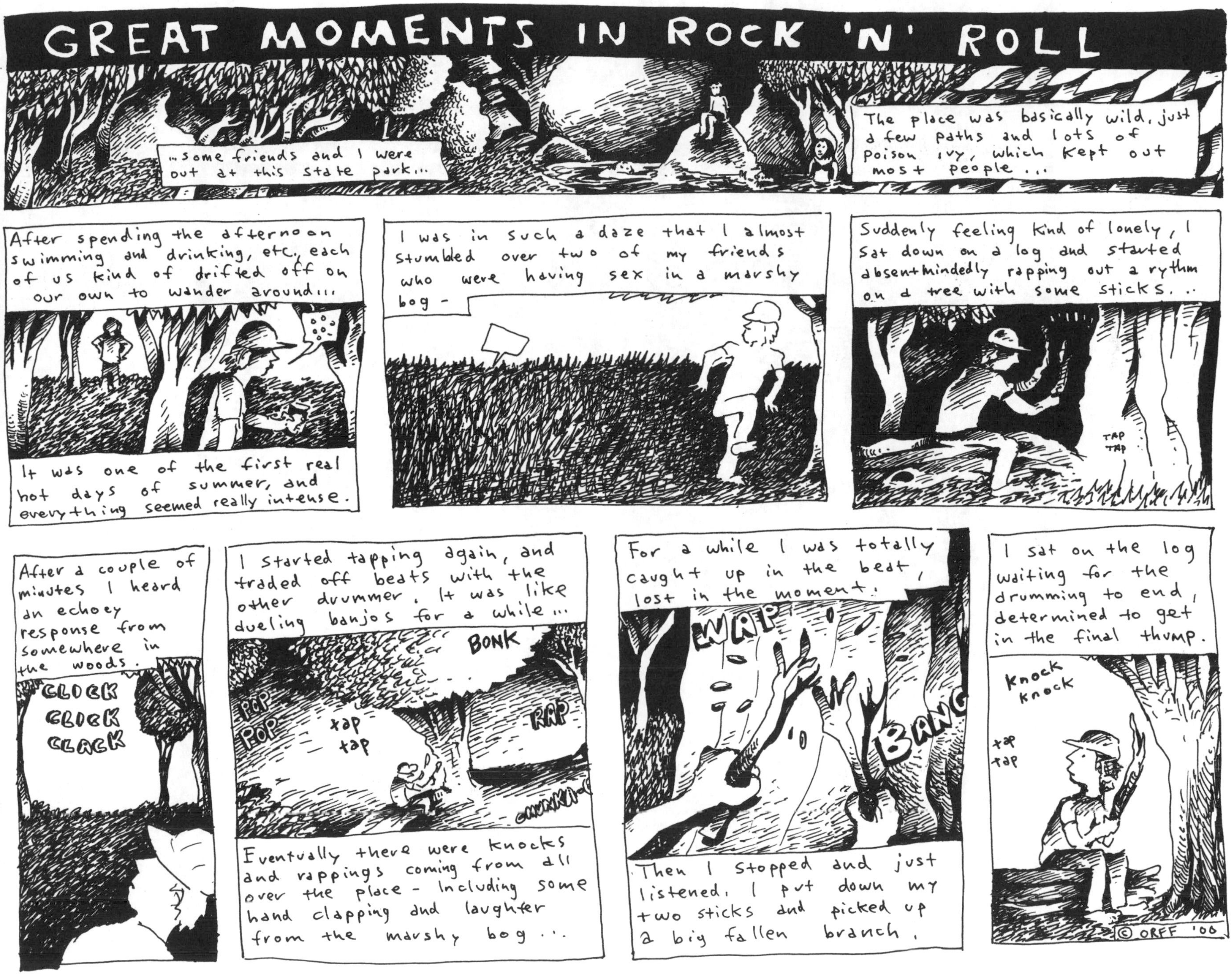
GREAT MOMENTS IN ROCK 'N' ROLL
...some friends and I were out at this state park...
The place was basically wild, just a few paths and lots of poison ivy, which kept out most people...
After spending the afternoon swimming and drinking, etc., each of us kind of drifted off on our own to wander around...
It was one of the first real hot days of summer, and everything seemed really intense.
I was in such a daze that I almost stumbled over two of my friends who were having sex in a marshy bog -
Suddenly feeling kind of lonely, I sat down on a log and started absentmindedly rapping out a rythm on a tree with some sticks...
TAP TAP
After a couple of minutes I heard an echoey response from somewhere in the woods.
CLICK CLICK CLACK
I started tapping again, and traded off beats with the other drummer. It was like dueling banjos for a while...
BONK
POP POP
tap tap
RAP
Eventually there were knocks and rappings coming from all over the place - Including some hand clapping and laughter from the marshy bog...
For a while I was totally caught up in the beat, lost in the moment.
WAP
BANG
Then I stopped and just listened. I put down my two sticks and picked up a big fallen branch.
I sat on the log waiting for the drumming to end, determined to get in the final thump.
knock knock
tap tap
© ORFF '00

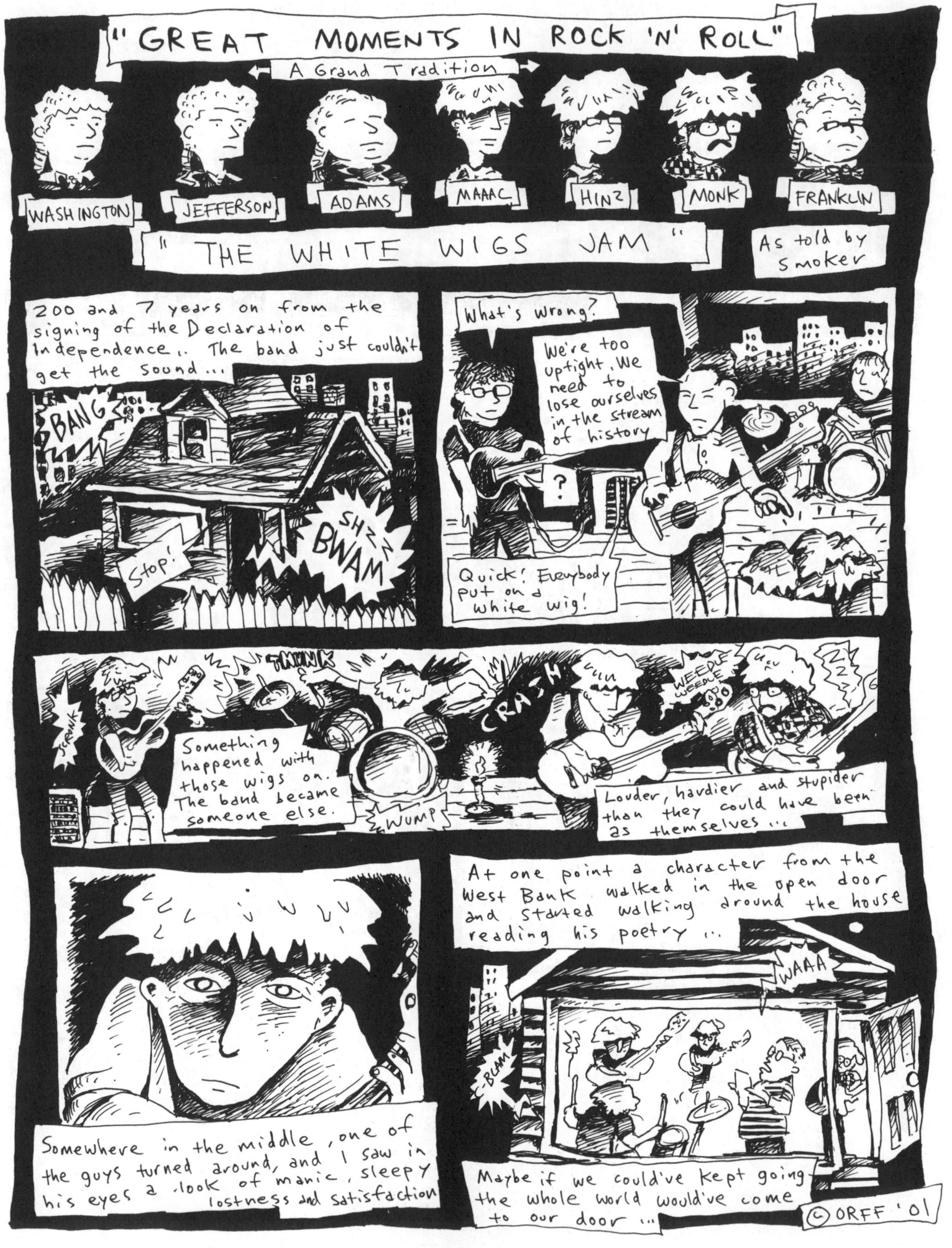
"GREAT MOMENTS IN ROCK 'N' ROLL"
A Grand Tradition
WASHINGTON
JEFFERSON
ADAMS
MAAAC
HINZ
MONK
FRANKLIN
"THE WHITE WIGS JAM"
As told by smoker
200 and 7 years on from the signing of the Declaration of Independence.. The band just couldn't get the sound...
BANG
Stop!
BWAM
What's wrong?
We're too uptight. We need to lose ourselves in the stream of history
?
Quick! Everybody put on a white wig!
CRASH
WEEDLE WEEDLE
Something happened with those wigs on. The band became someone else.
WUMP
Louder, hardier and stupider than they could have been as themselves...
Somewhere in the middle, one of the guys turned around, and I saw in his eyes a look of manic, sleepy lostness and satisfaction
At one point a character from the West Bank walked in the open door and started walking around the house reading his poetry..
WAAA
BLAM
Maybe if we could've kept going the whole world would've come to our door...
© ORFF '01

GREAT MOMENTS IN ROCK 'N' ROLL

As told by Yrs Truly

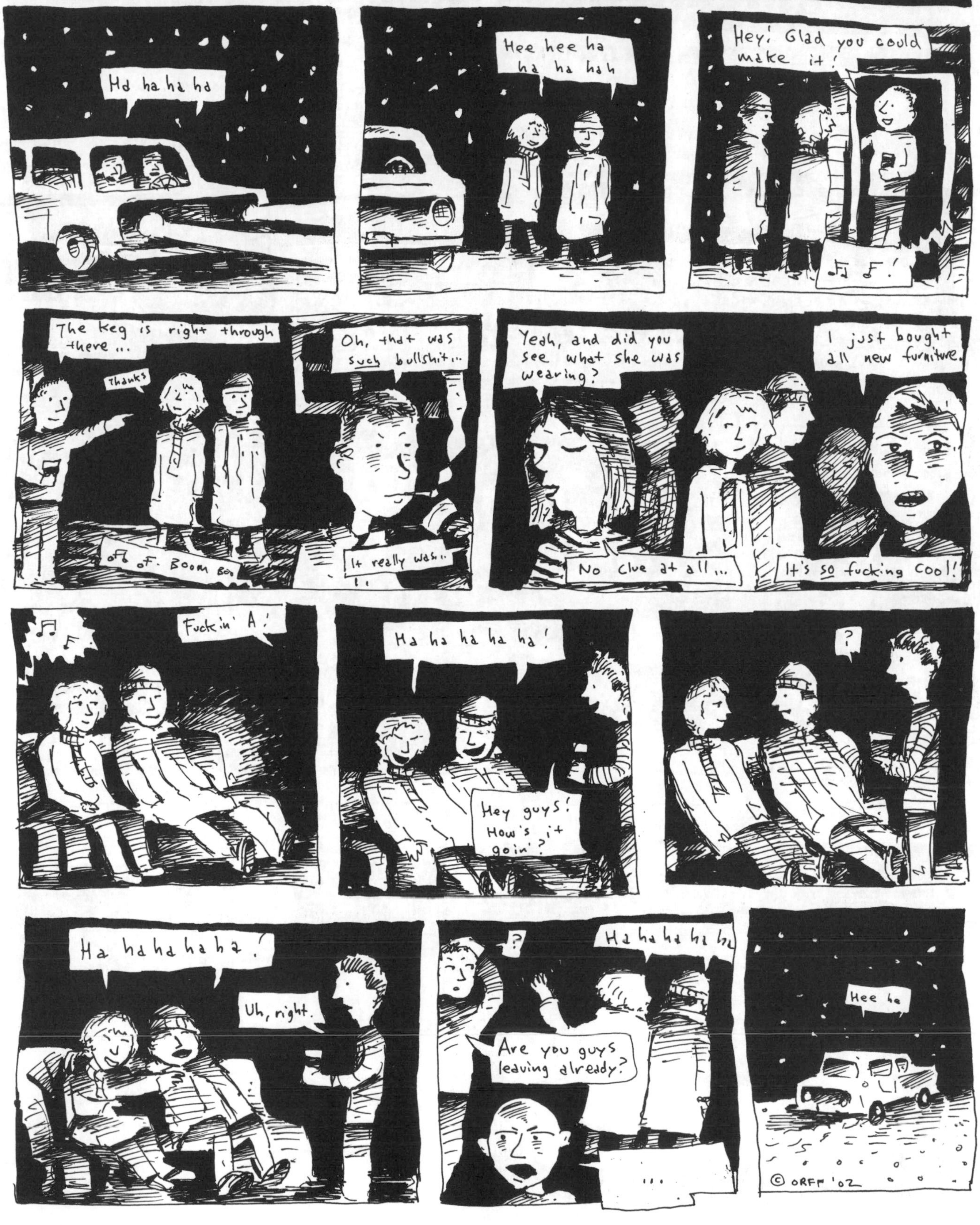

Ha ha ha ha
Hee hee ha ha ha hah
Hey! Glad you could make it!
The keg is right through there...
Thanks
ofb of. Boom Boo
Oh, that was such bullshit...
It really was...
Yeah, and did you see what she was wearing?
No clue at all...
I just bought all new furniture.
It's so fucking cool!
Fuckin' A!
Ha ha ha ha ha!
Hey guys! How's it goin'?
?
Ha hahahaha!
Uh, right.
?
Ha ha ha ha ha
Are you guys leaving already?
...
Hee ha
© ORFF '02

GREAT MOMENTS IN ROCK 'N' ROLL

As told by K.O.

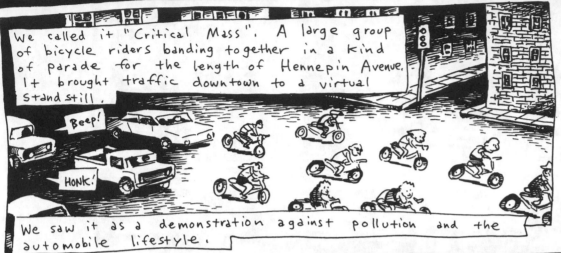

We called it "Critical Mass". A large group of bicycle riders banding together in a kind of parade for the length of Hennepin Avenue. It brought traffic downtown to a virtual standstill.

Beep!

HONK!

We saw it as a demonstration against pollution and the automobile lifestyle.

The day had been a success. A bunch of us went back to our apartment to celebrate.

After a few beers, a friend of mine had a brainstorm.

Forget "Critical Mass"...

It should be "Critical Ass"!

He proposed that we strip naked and bike over to "Hidden Beach."

A couple of us agreed.

It was around midnight when we headed out across the city...

You better not ditch me! I've got our clothes in my backpack!

We flew clear and free, without hassle.

Beep!

Lake of the Isles

When we got to the beach we found a group of people skinny-dipping.

It felt natural. I mean, we were already naked.

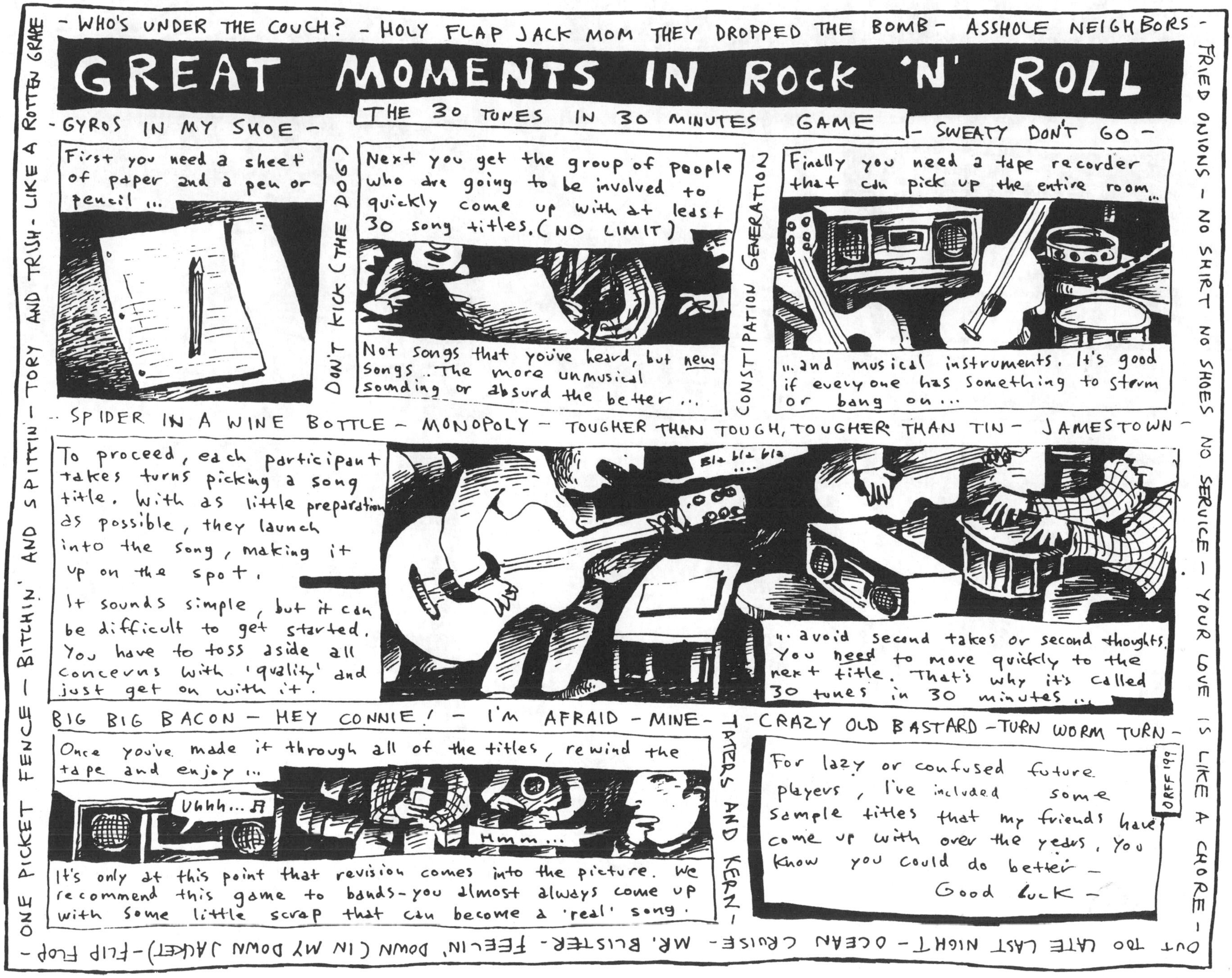

- WHO'S UNDER THE COUCH? - HOLY FLAP JACK MOM THEY DROPPED THE BOMB - ASSHOLE NEIGHBORS -
GREAT MOMENTS IN ROCK 'N' ROLL
THE 30 TUNES IN 30 MINUTES GAME
- GYROS IN MY SHOE -
- SWEATY DON'T GO -
First you need a sheet of paper and a pen or pencil ...
DON'T KICK (THE DOG)
Next you get the group of people who are going to be involved to quickly come up with at least 30 song titles. (NO LIMIT)
Not songs that you've heard, but new songs. The more unmusical sounding or absurd the better ...
CONSTIPATION GENERATION
Finally you need a tape recorder that can pick up the entire room ...
... and musical instruments. It's good if everyone has something to strum or bang on ...
- SPIDER IN A WINE BOTTLE - MONOPOLY - TOUGHER THAN TOUGH, TOUGHER THAN TIN - JAMESTOWN -
To proceed, each participant takes turns picking a song title. With as little preparation as possible, they launch into the song, making it up on the spot.
It sounds simple, but it can be difficult to get started. You have to toss aside all concerns with 'quality' and just get on with it.
Bla bla bla ....
... avoid second takes or second thoughts. You need to move quickly to the next title. That's why it's called 30 tunes in 30 minutes ...
BIG BIG BACON - HEY CONNIE! - I'M AFRAID - MINE - CRAZY OLD BASTARD - TURN WORM TURN -
Once you've made it through all of the titles, rewind the tape and enjoy ...
Uhhh... ♫
Hmm...
It's only at this point that revision comes into the picture. We recommend this game to bands - you almost always come up with some little scrap that can become a 'real' song.
TATERS AND KERN -
For lazy or confused future players, I've included some sample titles that my friends have come up with over the years. You know you could do better -
Good Luck -
ORFF 99
FRIED ONIONS - NO SHIRT NO SHOES NO SERVICE - YOUR LOVE IS LIKE A CHORE -
OUT TOO LATE LAST NIGHT - OCEAN CRUISE - MR. BLISTER - FEELIN' DOWN (IN MY DOWN JACKET) - FLIP FLOP -
ONE PICKET FENCE - BITCHIN' AND SPITTIN' - TORY AND TRISH - LIKE A ROTTEN GRAPE

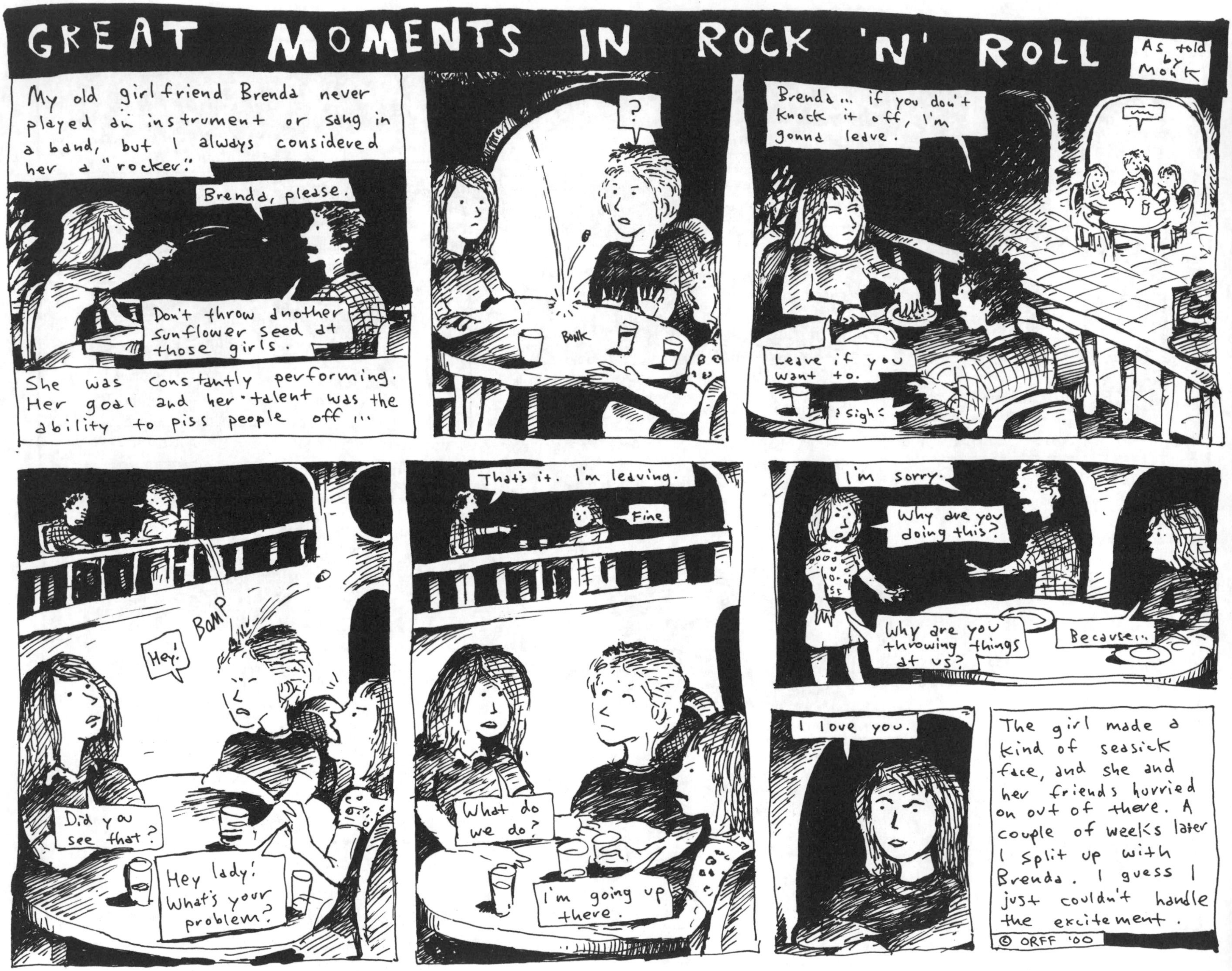
GREAT MOMENTS IN ROCK 'N' ROLL
As told by Monk
My old girlfriend Brenda never played an instrument or sang in a band, but I always considered her a "rocker."
Brenda, please.
Don't throw another sunflower seed at those girls.
She was constantly performing. Her goal and her talent was the ability to piss people off ...
?
BONK
Brenda ... if you don't knock it off, I'm gonna leave.
Leave if you want to.
{sigh}
Hey!
BOMP
Did you see that?
Hey lady! What's your problem?
That's it. I'm leaving.
Fine
What do we do?
I'm going up there.
I'm sorry.
Why are you doing this?
Why are you throwing things at us?
Because...
I love you.
The girl made a kind of seasick face, and she and her friends hurried on out of there. A couple of weeks later I split up with Brenda. I guess I just couldn't handle the excitement.
© ORFF '00

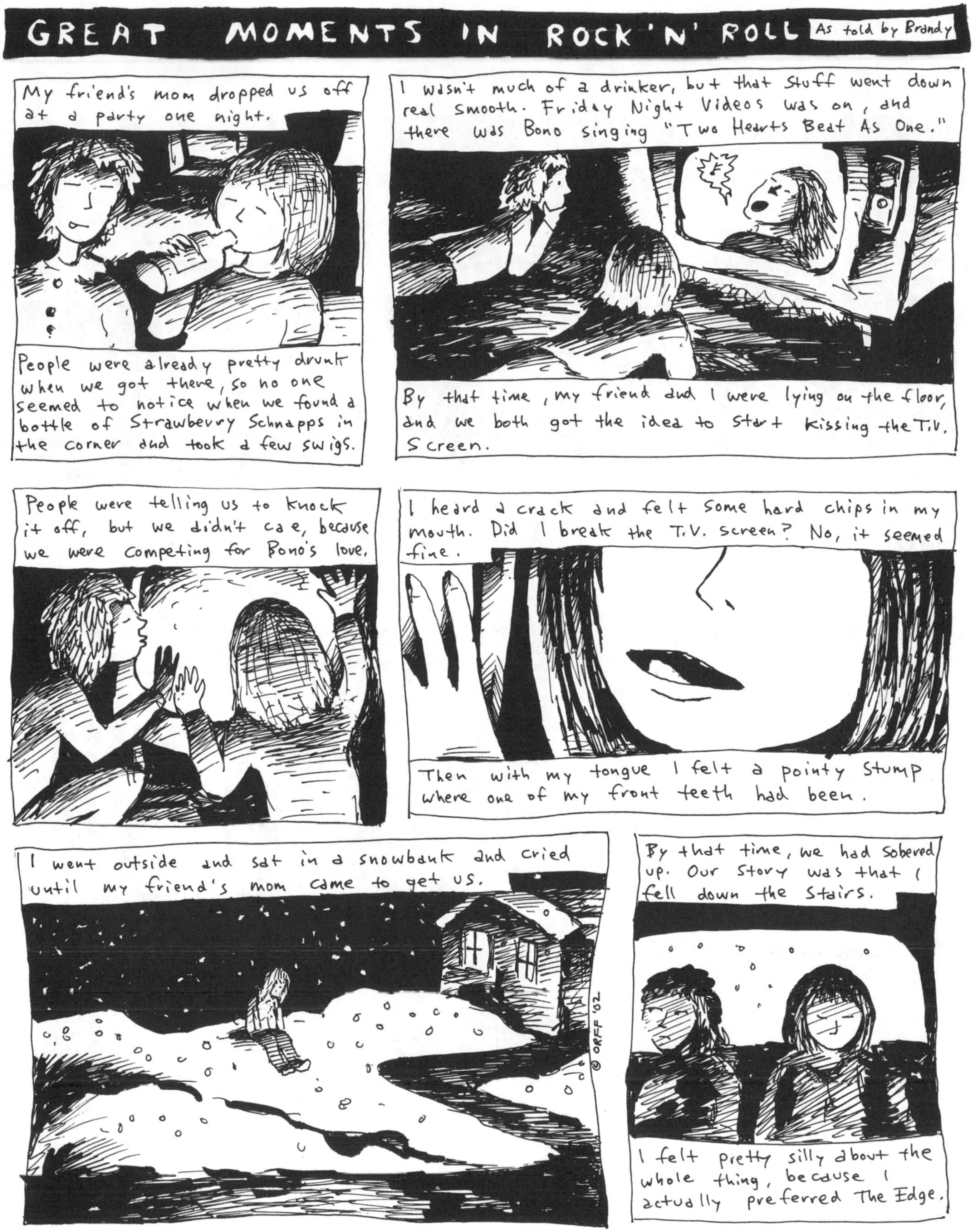
GREAT MOMENTS IN ROCK 'N' ROLL
As told by Brandy
My friend's mom dropped us off at a party one night.
People were already pretty drunk when we got there, so no one seemed to notice when we found a bottle of Strawberry Schnapps in the corner and took a few swigs.
I wasn't much of a drinker, but that stuff went down real smooth. Friday Night Videos was on, and there was Bono singing "Two Hearts Beat As One."
By that time, my friend and I were lying on the floor, and we both got the idea to start kissing the T.V. Screen.
People were telling us to knock it off, but we didn't cae, because we were competing for Bono's love.
I heard a crack and felt some hard chips in my mouth. Did I break the T.V. screen? No, it seemed fine.
Then with my tongue I felt a pointy stump where one of my front teeth had been.
I went outside and sat in a snowbank and cried until my friend's mom came to get us.
© ORFF '02
By that time, we had sobered up. Our story was that I fell down the stairs.
I felt pretty silly about the whole thing, because I actually preferred The Edge.

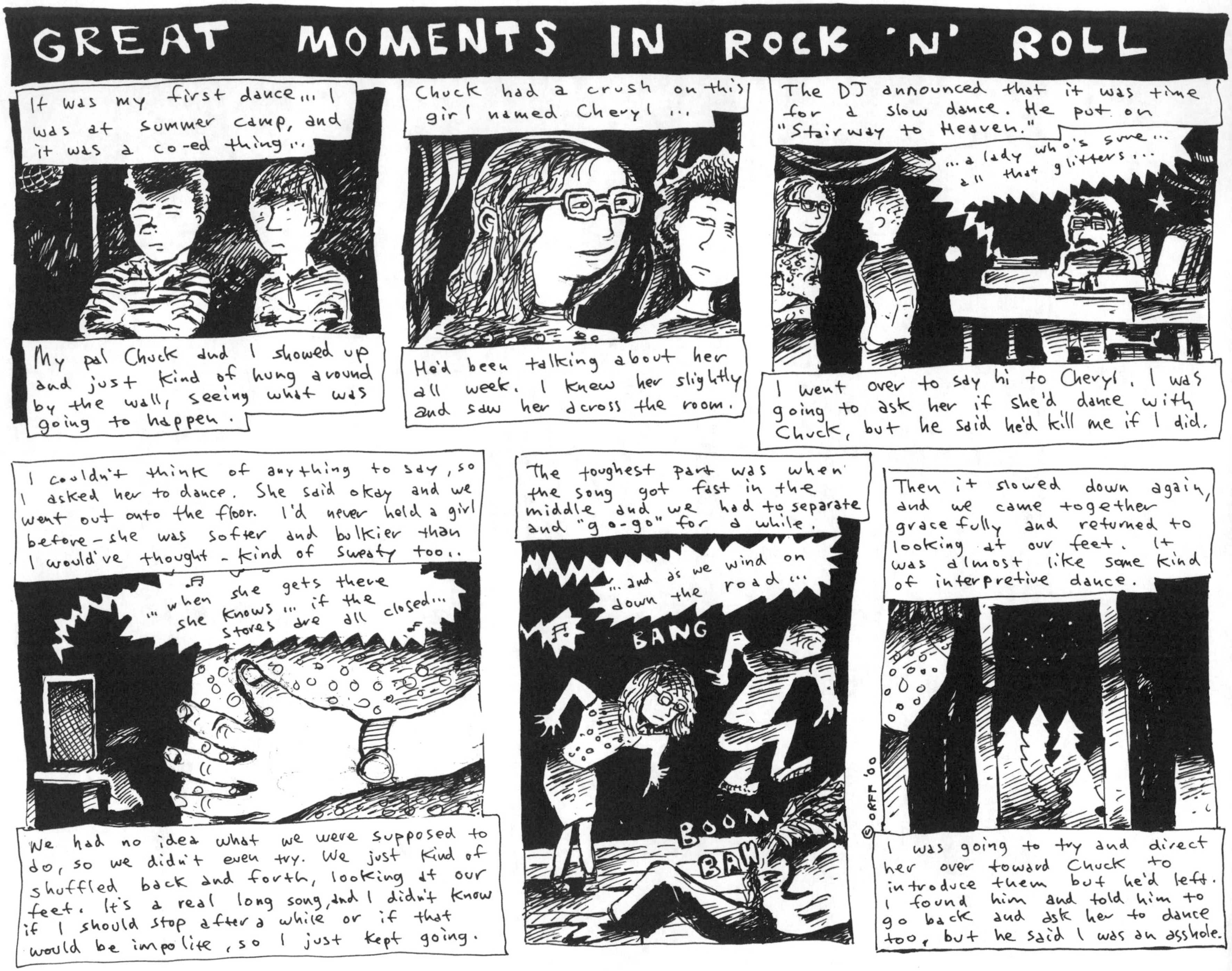
GREAT MOMENTS IN ROCK 'N' ROLL
It was my first dance... I was at summer camp, and it was a co-ed thing...
My pal Chuck and I showed up and just kind of hung around by the wall, seeing what was going to happen.
Chuck had a crush on this girl named Cheryl...
He'd been talking about her all week. I knew her slightly and saw her across the room.
The DJ announced that it was time for a slow dance. He put on "Stairway to Heaven."
...a lady who's sure... all that glitters...
I went over to say hi to Cheryl. I was going to ask her if she'd dance with Chuck, but he said he'd kill me if I did.
I couldn't think of anything to say, so I asked her to dance. She said okay and we went out onto the floor. I'd never held a girl before - she was softer and bulkier than I would've thought - kind of sweaty too..
...when she gets there she knows... if the stores are all closed...
We had no idea what we were supposed to do, so we didn't even try. We just kind of shuffled back and forth, looking at our feet. It's a real long song, and I didn't know if I should stop after a while or if that would be impolite, so I just kept going.
The toughest part was when the song got fast in the middle and we had to separate and "go-go" for a while.
...and as we wind on down the road...
BANG
BOOM
BAM
© ORFF '00
Then it slowed down again, and we came together gracefully and returned to looking at our feet. It was almost like some kind of interpretive dance.
I was going to try and direct her over toward Chuck to introduce them but he'd left. I found him and told him to go back and ask her to dance too, but he said I was an asshole.

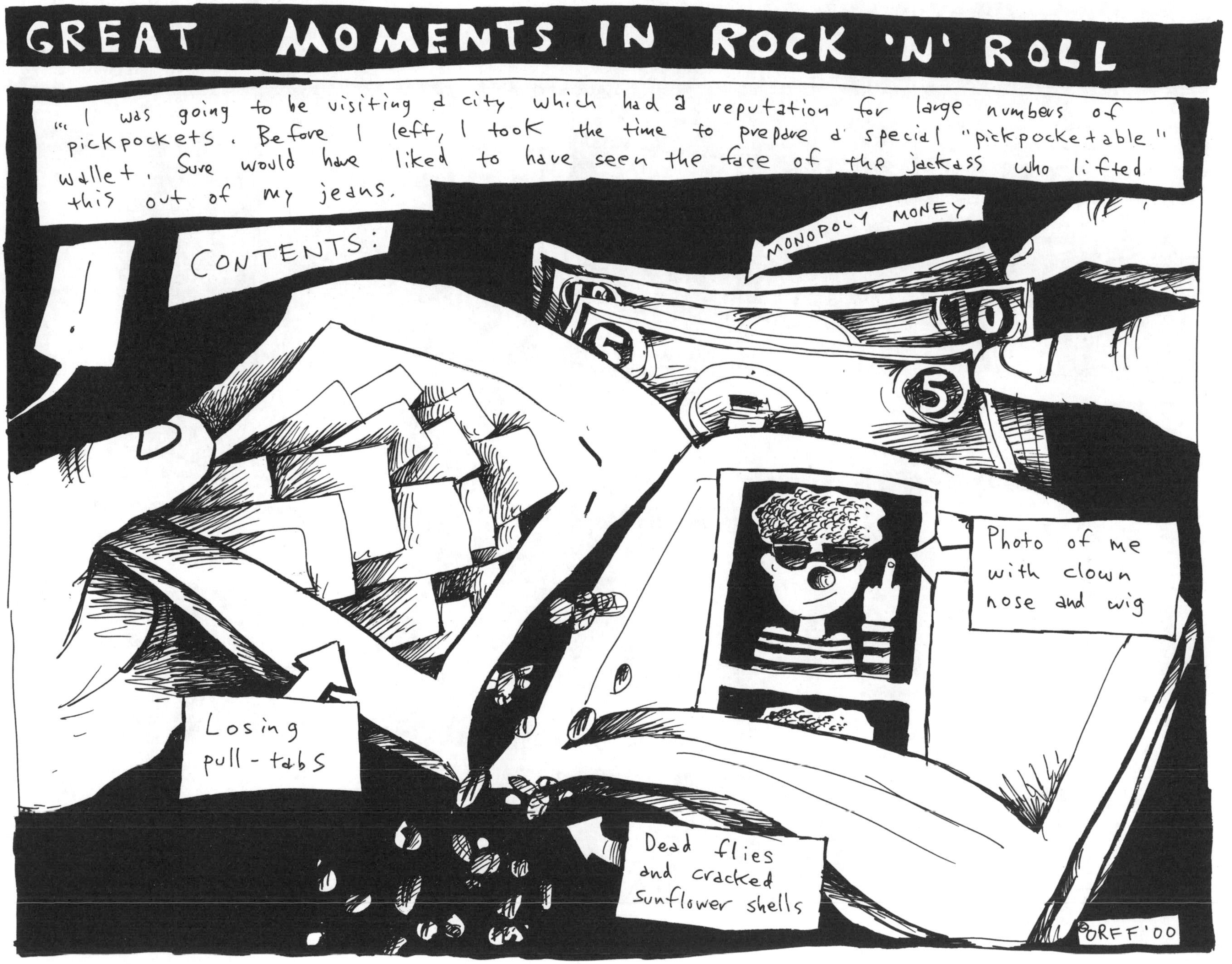
GREAT MOMENTS IN ROCK 'N' ROLL
"I was going to be visiting a city which had a reputation for large numbers of pickpockets. Before I left, I took the time to prepare a special "pickpocketable" wallet. Sure would have liked to have seen the face of the jackass who lifted this out of my jeans.
!
CONTENTS:
MONOPOLY MONEY
Photo of me with clown nose and wig
Losing pull-tabs
Dead flies and cracked sunflower shells
©ORFF '00

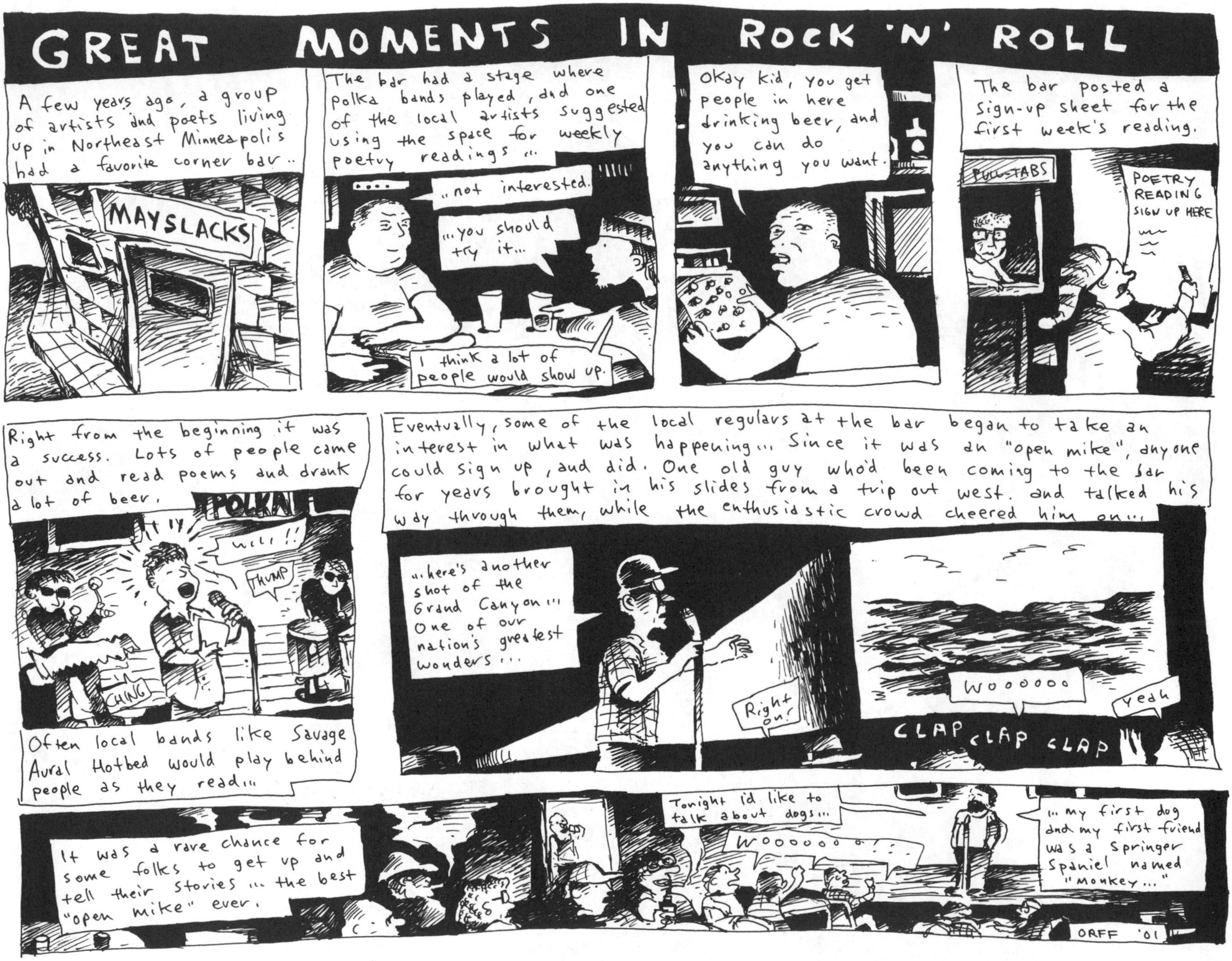
GREAT MOMENTS IN ROCK 'N' ROLL
A few years ago, a group of artists and poets living up in Northeast Minneapolis had a favorite corner bar..
MAYSLACKS
The bar had a stage where polka bands played, and one of the local artists suggested using the space for weekly poetry readings...
..not interested.
...you should try it...
I think a lot of people would show up.
Okay kid, you get people in here drinking beer, and you can do anything you want.
The bar posted a sign-up sheet for the first week's reading.
PULLTABS
POETRY READING SIGN UP HERE
Right from the beginning it was a success. Lots of people came out and read poems and drank a lot of beer.
POLKA
Well!!
THUMP
CHING
Often local bands like Savage Aural Hotbed would play behind people as they read...
Eventually, some of the local regulars at the bar began to take an interest in what was happening... Since it was an "open mike", anyone could sign up, and did. One old guy who'd been coming to the bar for years brought in his slides from a trip out west. and talked his way through them, while the enthusiastic crowd cheered him on...
..here's another shot of the Grand Canyon... One of our nation's greatest wonders...
Right on!
Wooooooo
Yeah
CLAP CLAP CLAP
It was a rare chance for some folks to get up and tell their stories ... the best "open mike" ever.
Tonight I'd like to talk about dogs...
Woooooooo!
... my first dog and my first friend was a Springer Spaniel named "Monkey..."
ORFF '01

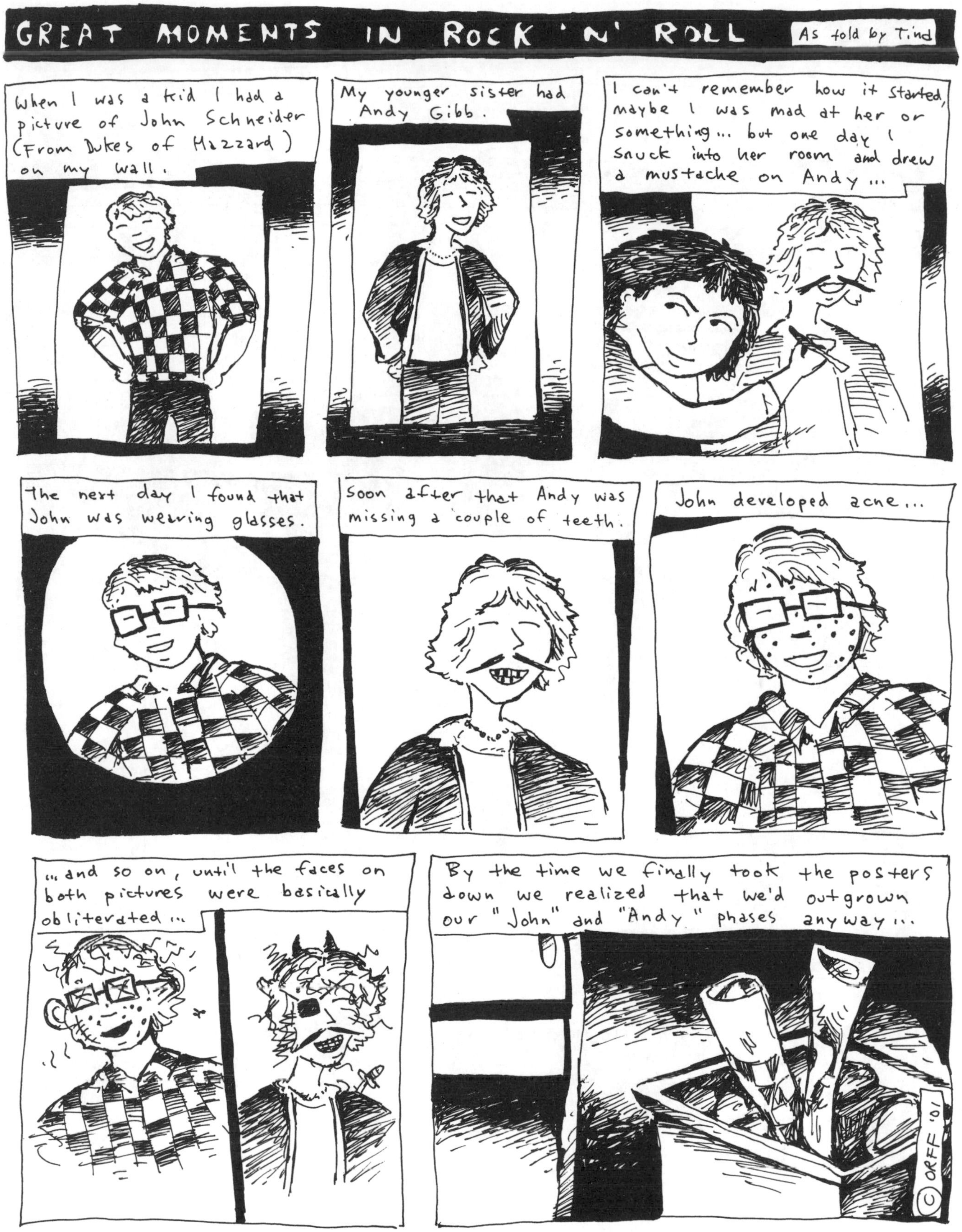
GREAT MOMENTS IN ROCK 'N' ROLL
As told by Tina
When I was a kid I had a picture of John Schneider (From Dukes of Hazzard) on my wall.
My younger sister had Andy Gibb.
I can't remember how it started, maybe I was mad at her or something... but one day I snuck into her room and drew a mustache on Andy...
The next day I found that John was wearing glasses.
Soon after that Andy was missing a couple of teeth.
John developed acne...
...and so on, until the faces on both pictures were basically obliterated...
By the time we finally took the posters down we realized that we'd outgrown our "John" and "Andy" phases anyway...
© ORFF '01

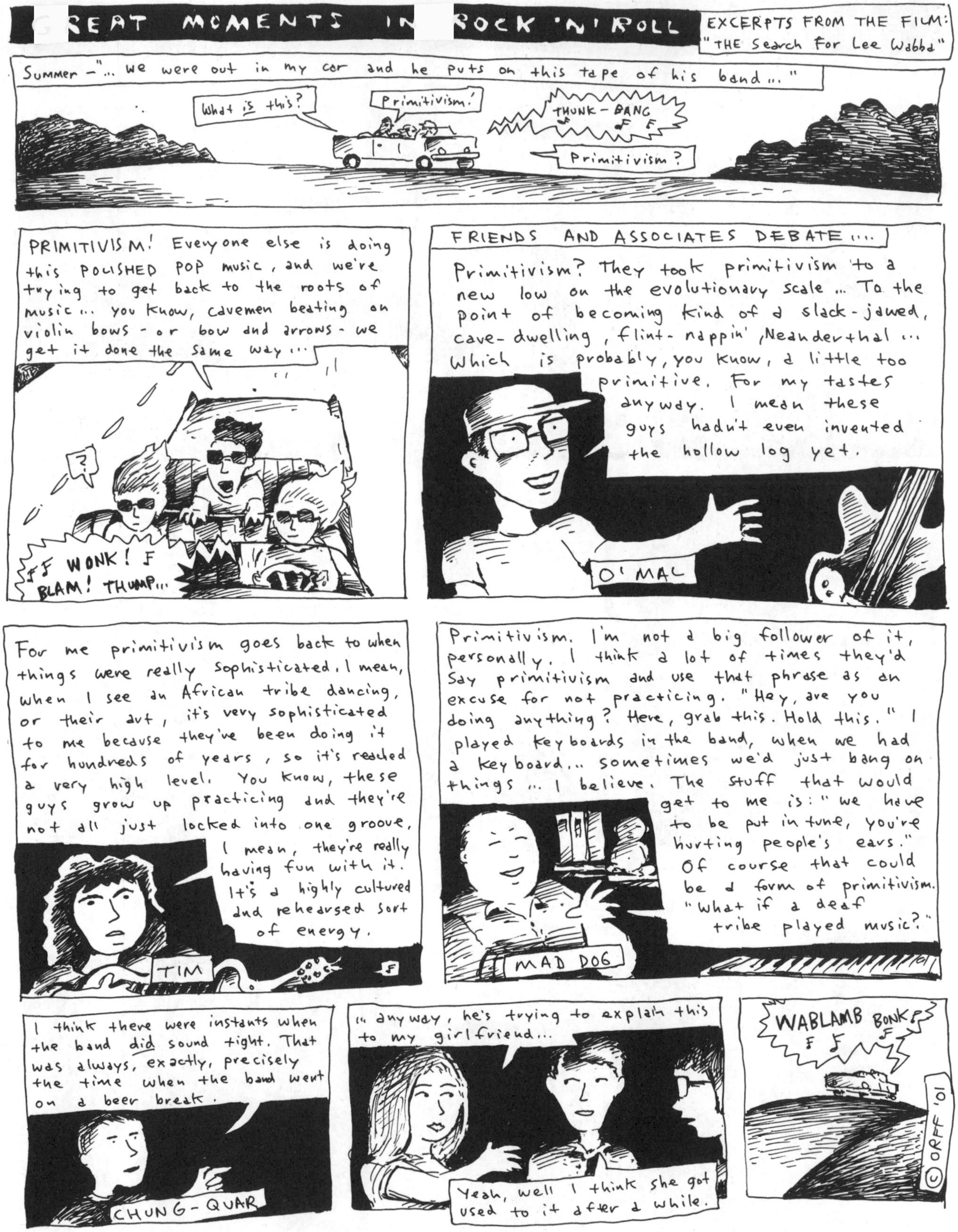

EAT MOMENTS IN OCK 'N' ROLL
EXCERPTS FROM THE FILM: "THE Search For Lee Wabbd"
Summer – "... we were out in my car and he puts on this tape of his band..."
What is this?
Primitivism!
THUNK-BANG
Primitivism?
PRIMITIVISM! Everyone else is doing this POLISHED POP music, and we're trying to get back to the roots of music... you know, cavemen beating on violin bows - or bow and arrows - we get it done the same way...
?
WONK! BLAM! THUMP...
FRIENDS AND ASSOCIATES DEBATE....
Primitivism? They took primitivism to a new low on the evolutionary scale... To the point of becoming kind of a slack-jawed, cave-dwelling, flint-nappin', Neanderthal... Which is probably, you know, a little too primitive. For my tastes anyway. I mean these guys hadn't even invented the hollow log yet.
O'MAL
For me primitivism goes back to when things were really sophisticated. I mean, when I see an African tribe dancing, or their art, it's very sophisticated to me because they've been doing it for hundreds of years, so it's reached a very high level. You know, these guys grow up practicing and they're not all just locked into one groove, I mean, they're really having fun with it. It's a highly cultured and rehearsed sort of energy.
TIM
Primitivism. I'm not a big follower of it, personally. I think a lot of times they'd say primitivism and use that phrase as an excuse for not practicing. "Hey, are you doing anything? Here, grab this. Hold this." I played keyboards in the band, when we had a keyboard... sometimes we'd just bang on things... I believe. The stuff that would get to me is: "we have to be put in tune, you're hurting people's ears." Of course that could be a form of primitivism. "What if a deaf tribe played music?"
MAD DOG
I think there were instants when the band did sound tight. That was always, exactly, precisely the time when the band went on a beer break.
CHUNG-QUAR
... anyway, he's trying to explain this to my girlfriend...
Yeah, well I think she got used to it after a while.
WABLAMB BONK
© ORFF '01

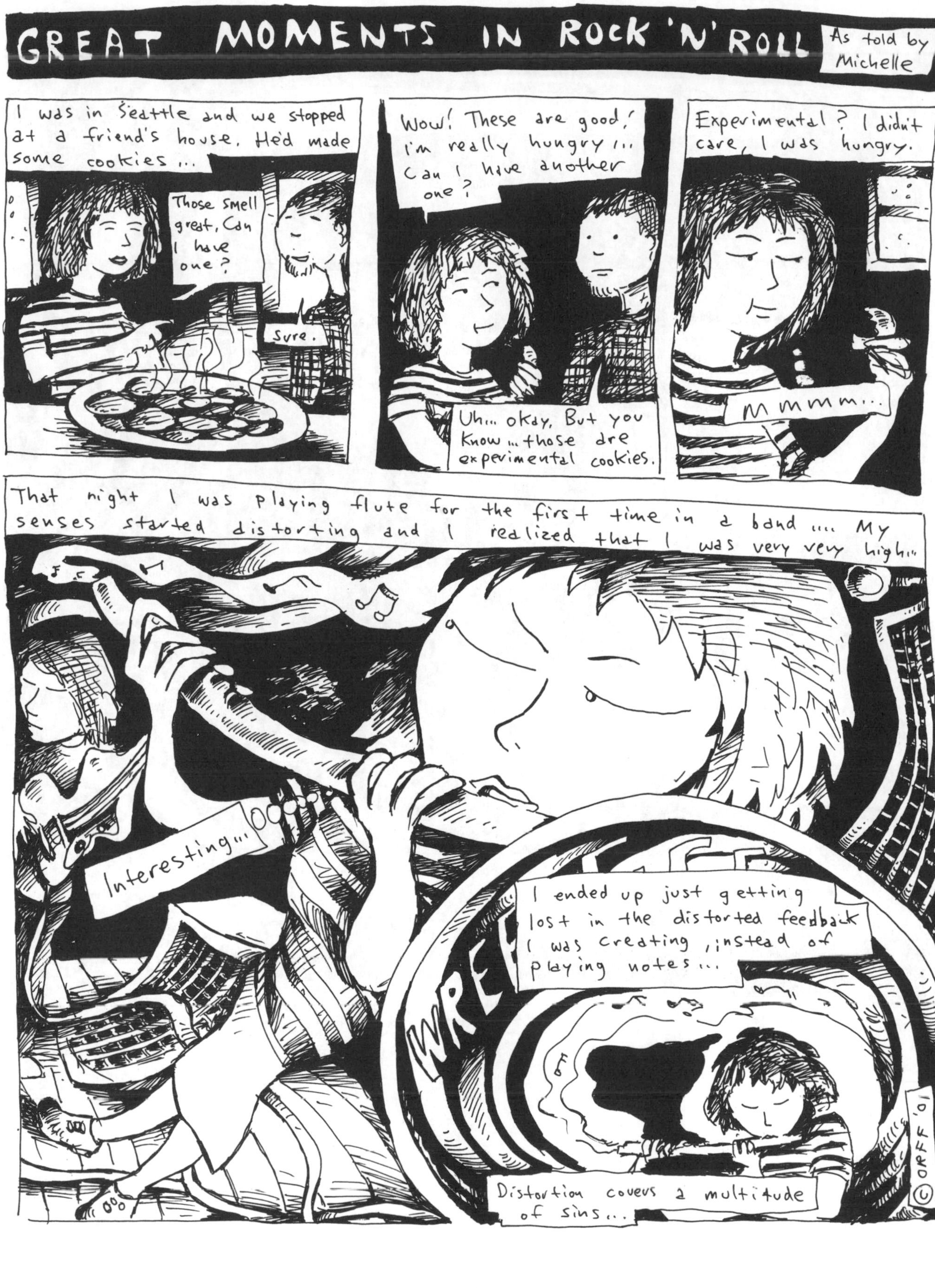
GREAT MOMENTS IN ROCK 'N' ROLL
As told by Michelle
I was in Seattle and we stopped at a friend's house. He'd made some cookies...
Those smell great, Can I have one?
Sure.
Wow! These are good! I'm really hungry... Can I have another one?
Uh... okay. But you know... those are experimental cookies.
Experimental? I didn't care, I was hungry.
MMMMM...
That night I was playing flute for the first time in a band.... My senses started distorting and I realized that I was very very high...
Interesting...
I ended up just getting lost in the distorted feedback I was creating, instead of playing notes...
WREE
Distortion covers a multitude of sins...
© ORFF '01

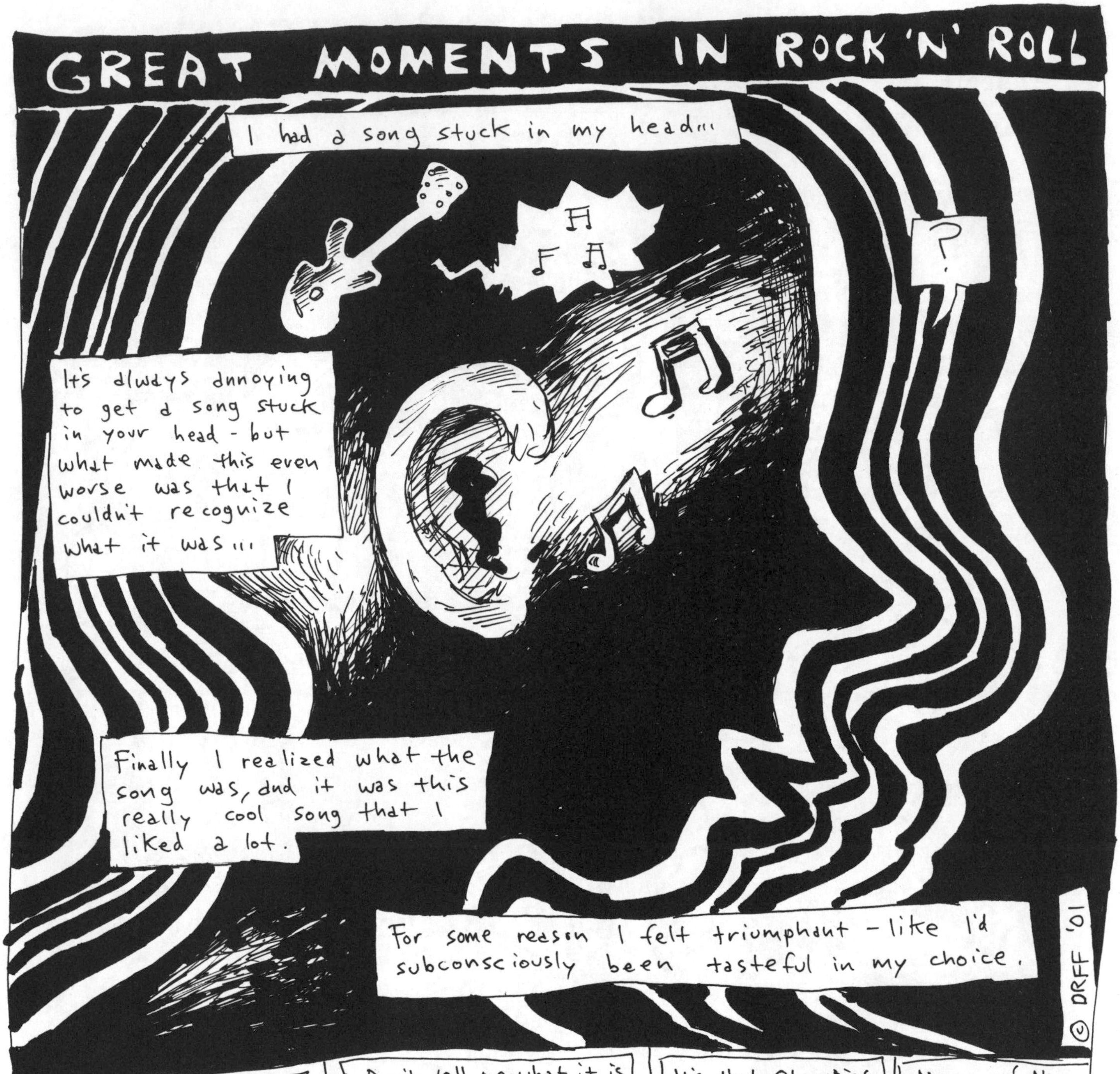
GREAT MOMENTS IN ROCK 'N' ROLL
I had a song stuck in my head...
?
It's always annoying to get a song stuck in your head - but what made this even worse was that I couldn't recognize what it was...
Finally I realized what the song was, and it was this really cool song that I liked a lot.
For some reason I felt triumphant - like I'd subconsciously been tasteful in my choice.
© DRFF '01

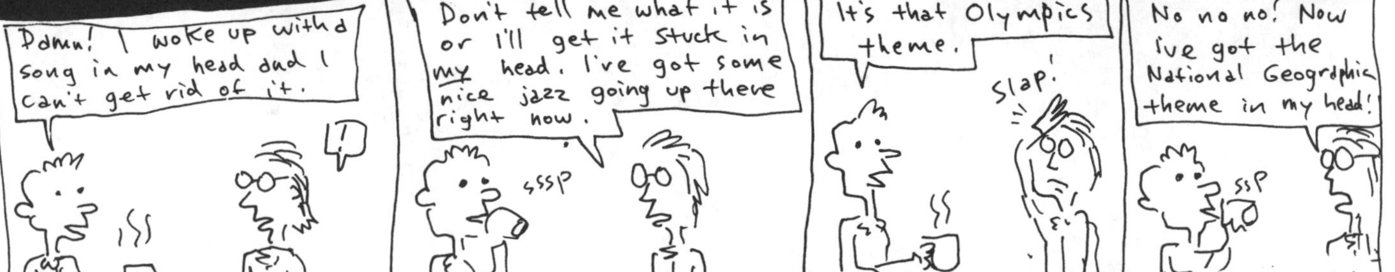
Damn! I woke up with a song in my head and I can't get rid of it.
!
Don't tell me what it is or I'll get it stuck in my head. I've got some nice jazz going up there right now.
SSSP
It's that Olympics theme.
SLAP!
No no no! Now I've got the National Geographic theme in my head!
SSP

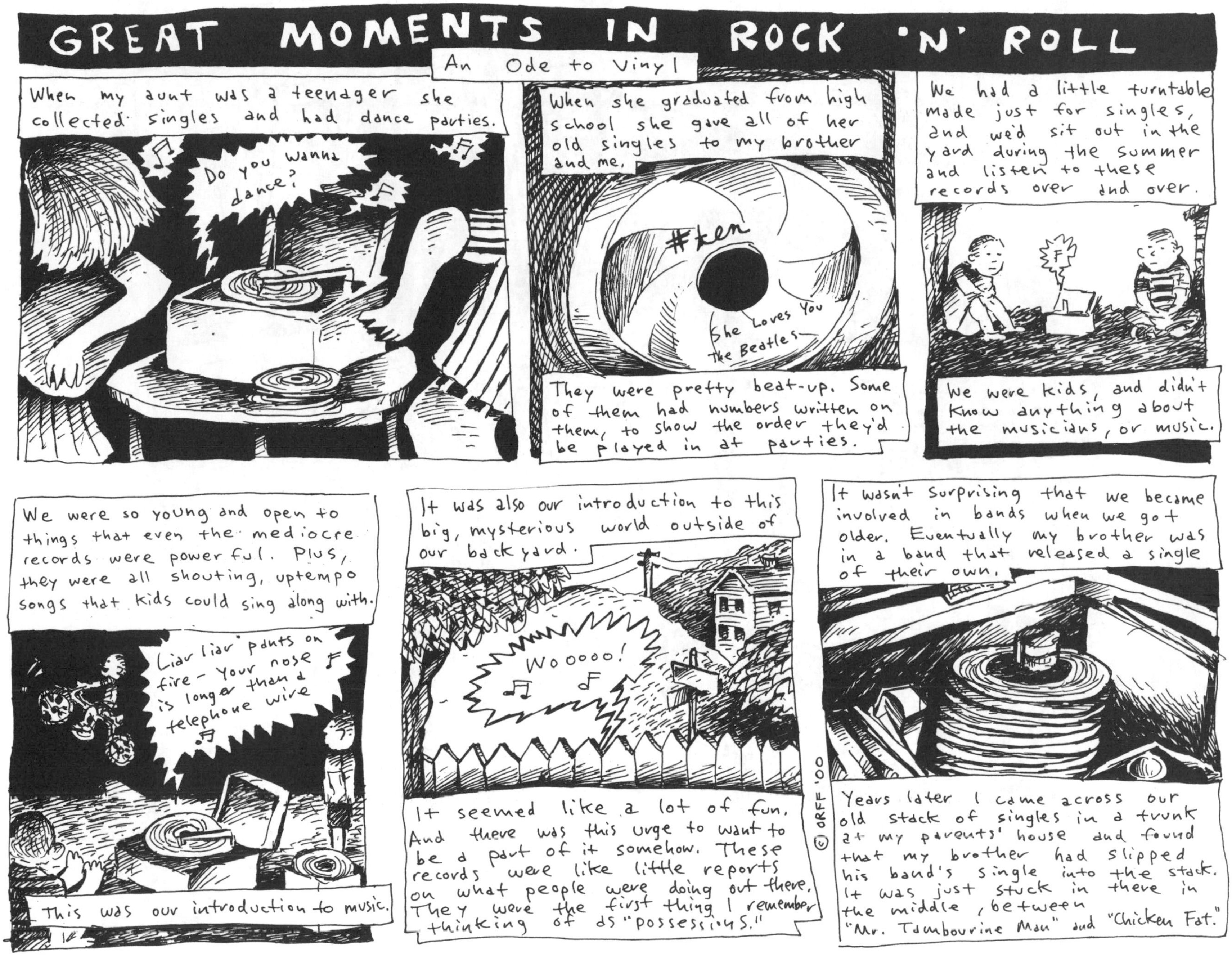
GREAT MOMENTS IN ROCK 'N' ROLL
An Ode to Vinyl
When my aunt was a teenager she collected singles and had dance parties.
Do you wanna dance?
When she graduated from high school she gave all of her old singles to my brother and me.
#ken
She Loves You
The Beatles
They were pretty beat-up. Some of them had numbers written on them, to show the order they'd be played in at parties.
We had a little turntable made just for singles, and we'd sit out in the yard during the summer and listen to these records over and over.
We were kids, and didn't know anything about the musicians, or music.
We were so young and open to things that even the mediocre records were powerful. Plus, they were all shouting, uptempo songs that kids could sing along with.
Liar liar pants on fire - Your nose is longer than a telephone wire
This was our introduction to music.
It was also our introduction to this big, mysterious world outside of our backyard.
Wooooo!
It seemed like a lot of fun. And there was this urge to want to be a part of it somehow. These records were like little reports on what people were doing out there. They were the first thing I remember thinking of as "possessions."
© ORFF '00
It wasn't surprising that we became involved in bands when we got older. Eventually my brother was in a band that released a single of their own.
Years later I came across our old stack of singles in a trunk at my parents' house and found that my brother had slipped his band's single into the stack. It was just stuck in there in the middle, between "Mr. Tambourine Man" and "Chicken Fat."

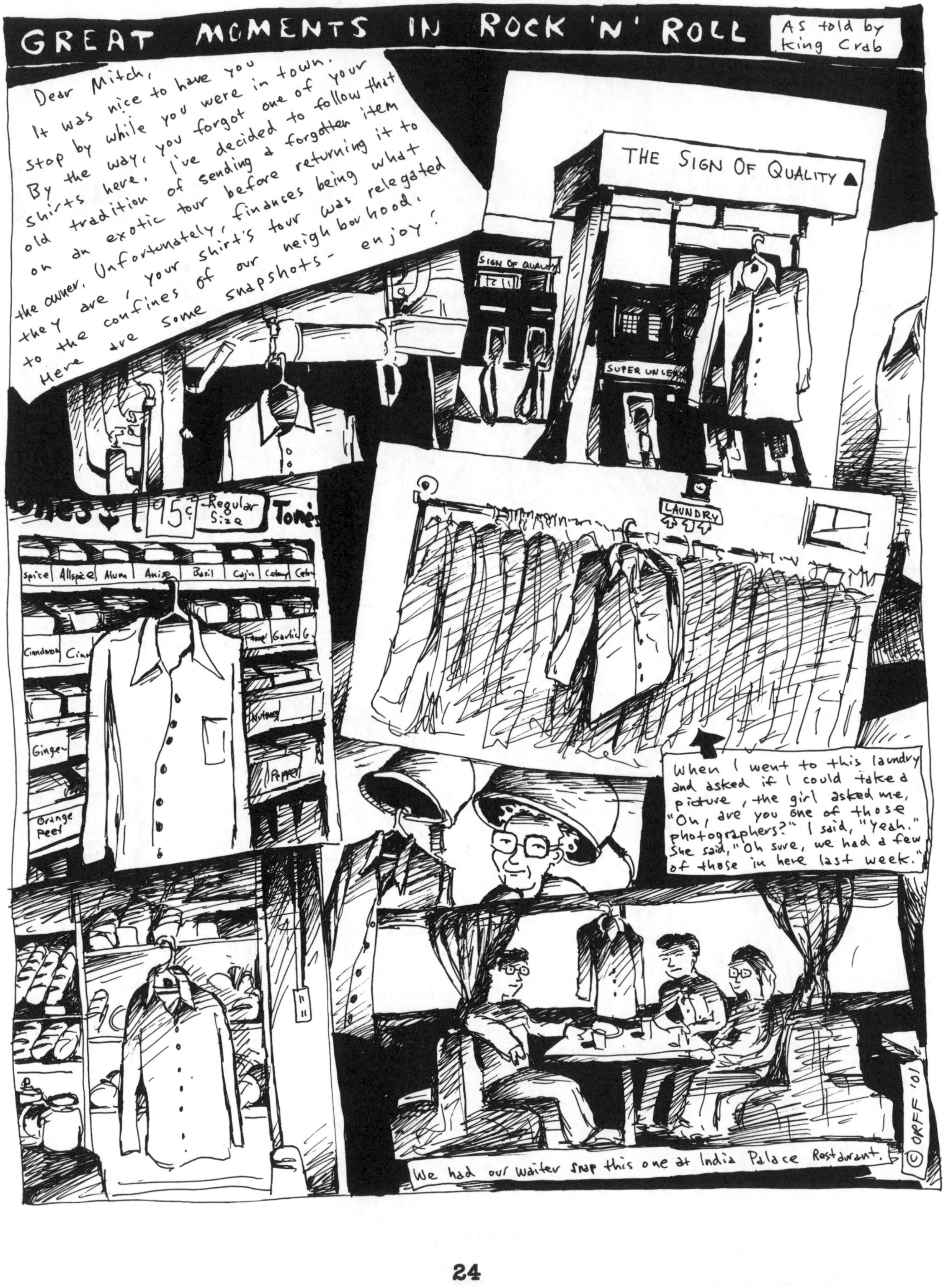

GREAT MOMENTS IN ROCK 'N' ROLL
As told by King Crab
Dear Mitch,
It was nice to have you stop by while you were in town. By the way, you forgot one of your shirts here. I've decided to follow that old tradition of sending a forgotten item on an exotic tour before returning it to the owner. Unfortunately, finances being what they are, your shirt's tour was relegated to the confines of our neighborhood. Here are some snapshots - enjoy!
THE SIGN OF QUALITY
SIGN OF QUALITY
SUPER UNLEADED
95¢ Regular Size
Tone's
Spice
Allspice
Alum
Anise
Basil
Cajun
Celery
Cinnamon
Garlic
Ginger
Nutmeg
Pepper
Orange Peel
LAUNDRY
When I went to this laundry and asked if I could take a picture, the girl asked me, "Oh, are you one of those photographers?" I said, "Yeah." She said, "Oh sure, we had a few of those in here last week."
We had our waiter snap this one at India Palace Restaurant.
© ORFF '01

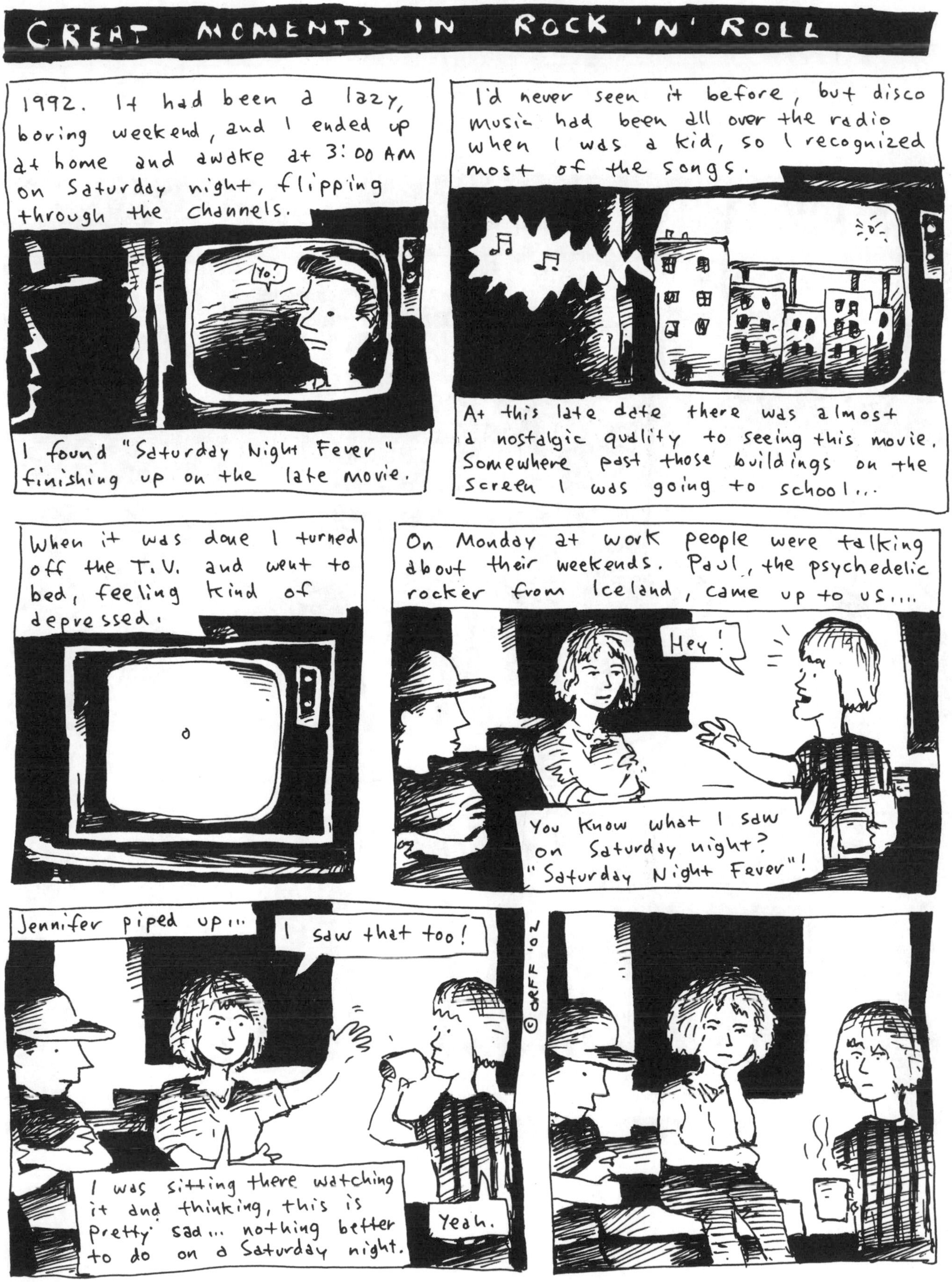
GREAT MOMENTS IN ROCK 'N' ROLL
1992. It had been a lazy, boring weekend, and I ended up at home and awake at 3:00 AM on Saturday night, flipping through the channels.
Yo!
I found "Saturday Night Fever" finishing up on the late movie.
I'd never seen it before, but disco music had been all over the radio when I was a kid, so I recognized most of the songs.
At this late date there was almost a nostalgic quality to seeing this movie. Somewhere past those buildings on the screen I was going to school...
When it was done I turned off the T.V. and went to bed, feeling kind of depressed.
On Monday at work people were talking about their weekends. Paul, the psychedelic rocker from Iceland, came up to us....
Hey!
You know what I saw on Saturday night? "Saturday Night Fever"!
Jennifer piped up...
I saw that too!
I was sitting there watching it and thinking, this is pretty sad... nothing better to do on a Saturday night.
Yeah.
© JEFF '02

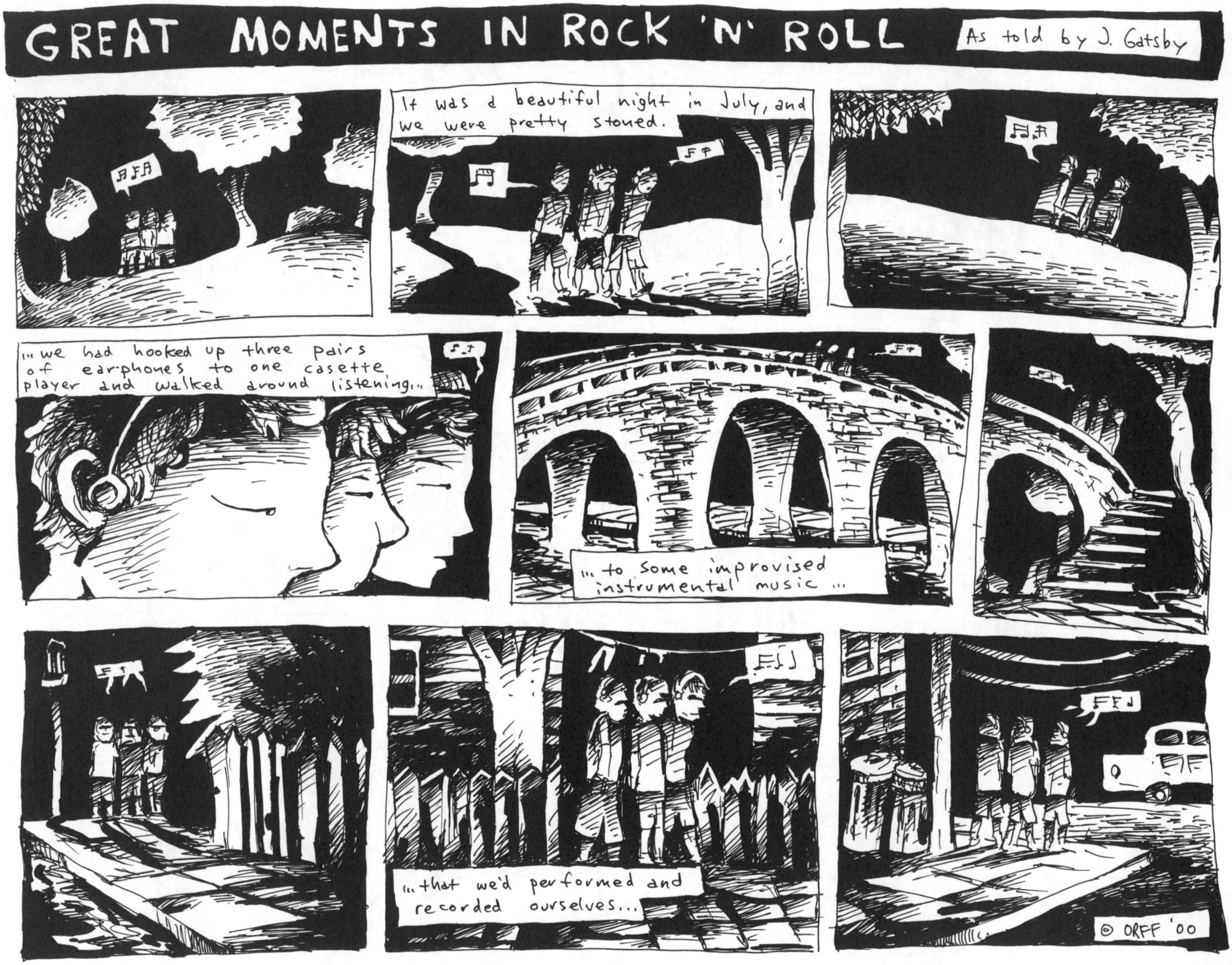
GREAT MOMENTS IN ROCK 'N' ROLL
As told by J. Gatsby
It was a beautiful night in July, and we were pretty stoned.
...we had hooked up three pairs of earphones to one casette player and walked around listening...
...to some improvised instrumental music...
...that we'd performed and recorded ourselves...
© ORFF '00

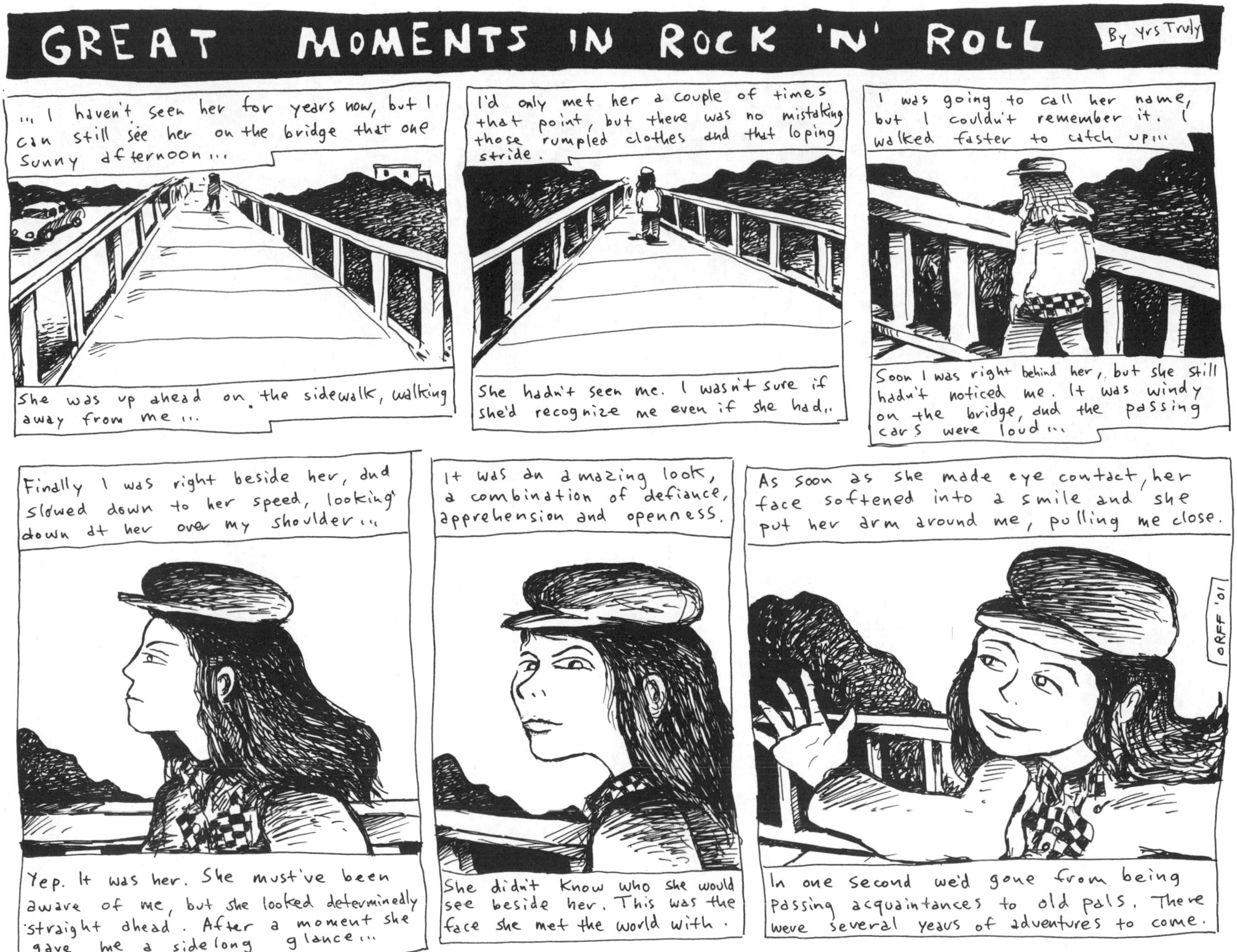
GREAT MOMENTS IN ROCK 'N' ROLL
By Yrs Truly
... I haven't seen her for years now, but I can still see her on the bridge that one sunny afternoon...
She was up ahead on the sidewalk, walking away from me...
I'd only met her a couple of times that point, but there was no mistaking those rumpled clothes and that loping stride.
She hadn't seen me. I wasn't sure if she'd recognize me even if she had..
I was going to call her name, but I couldn't remember it. I walked faster to catch up...
Soon I was right behind her, but she still hadn't noticed me. It was windy on the bridge, and the passing cars were loud...
Finally I was right beside her, and slowed down to her speed, looking down at her over my shoulder...
Yep. It was her. She must've been aware of me, but she looked determinedly straight ahead. After a moment she gave me a sidelong glance...
It was an amazing look, a combination of defiance, apprehension and openness.
She didn't know who she would see beside her. This was the face she met the world with.
As soon as she made eye contact, her face softened into a smile and she put her arm around me, pulling me close.
ORFF '01
In one second we'd gone from being passing acquaintances to old pals. There were several years of adventures to come.

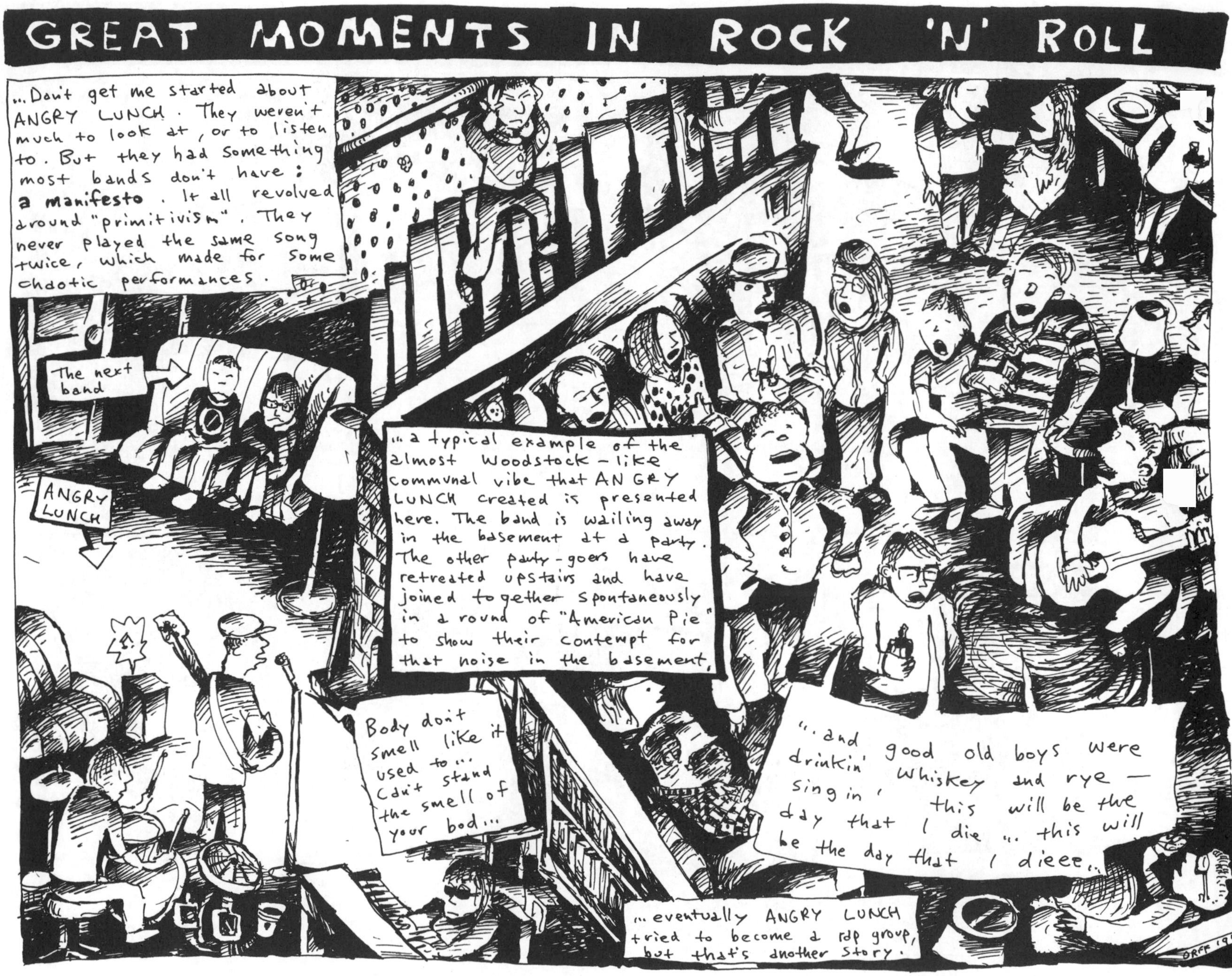
GREAT MOMENTS IN ROCK 'N' ROLL
...Don't get me started about ANGRY LUNCH. They weren't much to look at, or to listen to. But they had something most bands don't have: **a manifesto**. It all revolved around "primitivism". They never played the same song twice, which made for some chaotic performances.
The next band
ANGRY LUNCH
...a typical example of the almost Woodstock-like communal vibe that ANGRY LUNCH created is presented here. The band is wailing away in the basement at a party. The other party-goers have retreated upstairs and have joined together spontaneously in a round of "American Pie" to show their contempt for that noise in the basement.
Body don't smell like it used to... Can't stand the smell of your bod...
"...and good old boys were drinkin' whiskey and rye — singin' this will be the day that I die... this will be the day that I dieee..
...eventually ANGRY LUNCH tried to become a rap group, but that's another story.
ORFF '99

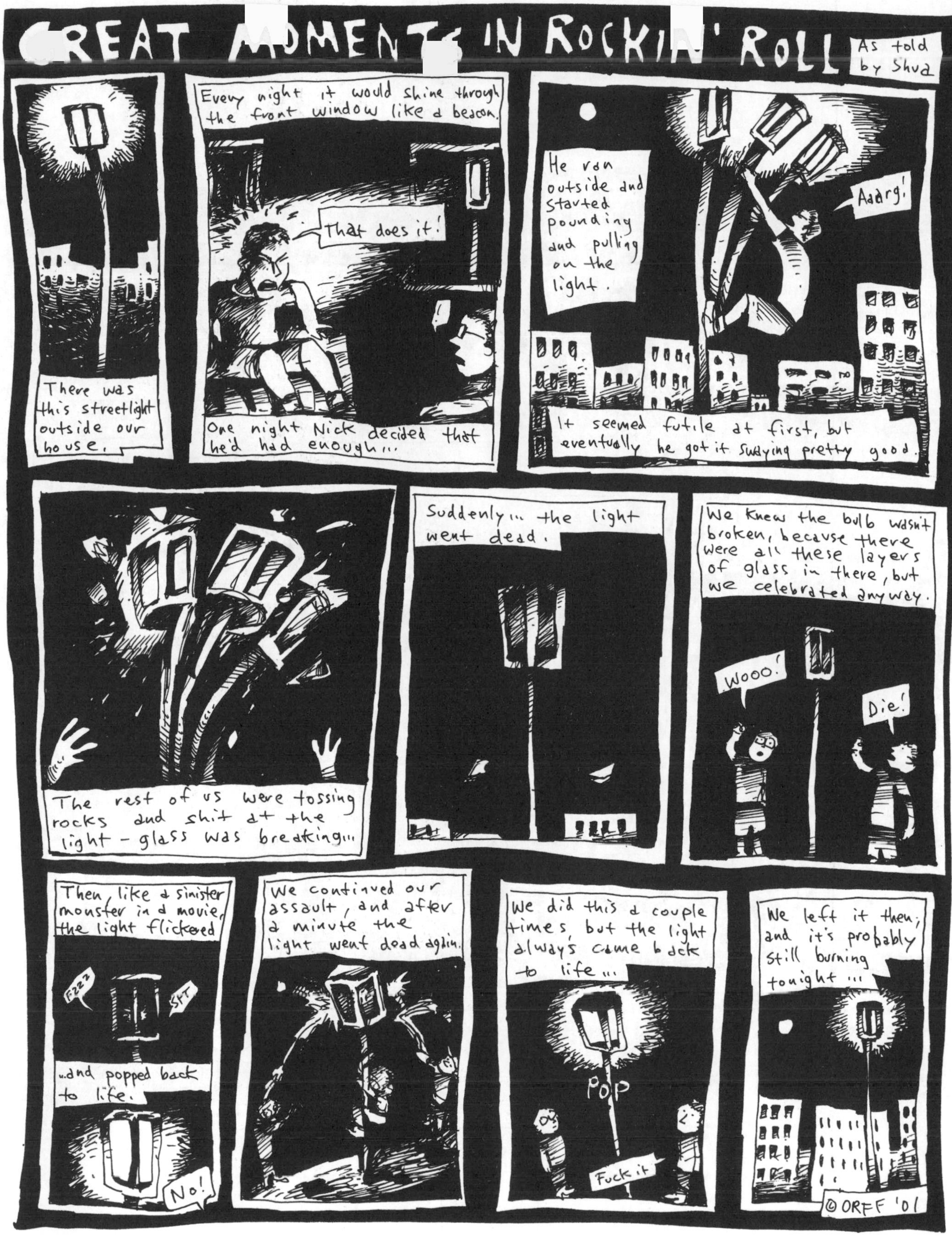
GREAT MOMENTS IN ROCKIN' ROLL
As told by Shua
There was this streetlight outside our house.
Every night it would shine through the front window like a beacon.
That does it!
One night Nick decided that he'd had enough...
He ran outside and started pounding and pulling on the light.
Aarg!
It seemed futile at first, but eventually he got it swaying pretty good.
The rest of us were tossing rocks and shit at the light - glass was breaking...
Suddenly... the light went dead.
We knew the bulb wasn't broken, because there were all these layers of glass in there, but we celebrated anyway.
Wooo!
Die!
Then, like a sinister monster in a movie, the light flickered
FZZZ
SFT
...and popped back to life.
No!
We continued our assault, and after a minute the light went dead again.
We did this a couple times, but the light always came back to life...
POP
Fuck it
We left it then; and it's probably still burning tonight...
© ORFF '01

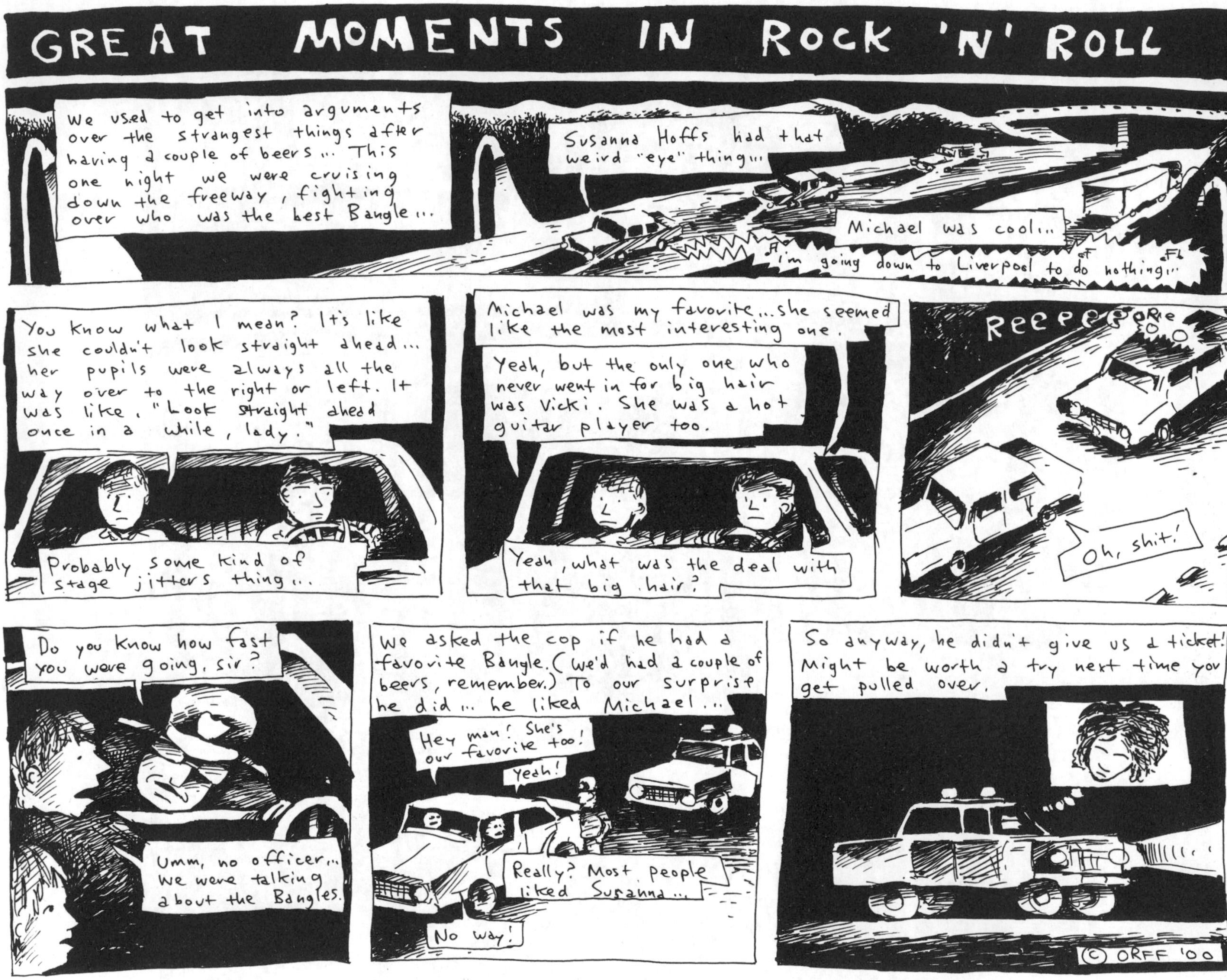
GREAT MOMENTS IN ROCK 'N' ROLL
We used to get into arguments over the strangest things after having a couple of beers... This one night we were cruising down the freeway, fighting over who was the best Bangle...
Susanna Hoffs had that weird "eye" thing...
Michael was cool...
I'm going down to Liverpool to do nothing...
You know what I mean? It's like she couldn't look straight ahead... her pupils were always all the way over to the right or left. It was like, "Look straight ahead once in a while, lady."
Probably some kind of stage jitters thing...
Michael was my favorite... she seemed like the most interesting one.
Yeah, but the only one who never went in for big hair was Vicki. She was a hot guitar player too.
Yeah, what was the deal with that big hair?
REEEEOOO
Oh, shit!
Do you know how fast you were going, sir?
Umm, no officer... We were talking about the Bangles.
We asked the cop if he had a favorite Bangle. (We'd had a couple of beers, remember.) To our surprise he did... he liked Michael...
Hey man! She's our favorite too!
Yeah!
Really? Most people liked Susanna...
No way!
So anyway, he didn't give us a ticket! Might be worth a try next time you get pulled over.
© ORFF '00

GREAT MOMENTS IN ROCK 'N' ROLL

Mac was one of those guys who made everything fun. He's got a little bit of Tom Sawyer in him,...

EXAMPLE: The time he invited us to his folks' cabin and we spent the day taking in the dock. THE POINT: He said it would be fun, and it was!

ANOTHER EXAMPLE: Mac would call up and get us to go out and see blues bands. None of us were really into the blues.

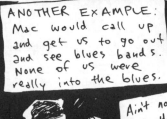

Ain't nothin' but the blues, baby!

One night he told us about a living legend, Albert Collins, who was going to be playing at the old Union Bar.

We all got there before Mac...

Yeah... Yeah.

Albert Collins lived up to his reputation, he was fantastic...

...he used this super long guitar cord, so that he could leave the stage and walk around the bar while he played this long solo...

I kind of followed him out past the pool tables, looking for Mac.

Albert ended up out on the sidewalk, still playing his solo, but all the sound came from inside...

I remember thinking "Mac would love this."

Then, there he was! Coming up the street.

UNION

Hey mac!

Hey mac!

Hey! It's Albert Collins!

That was my favorite part of the show

wow!

© ORFF '00

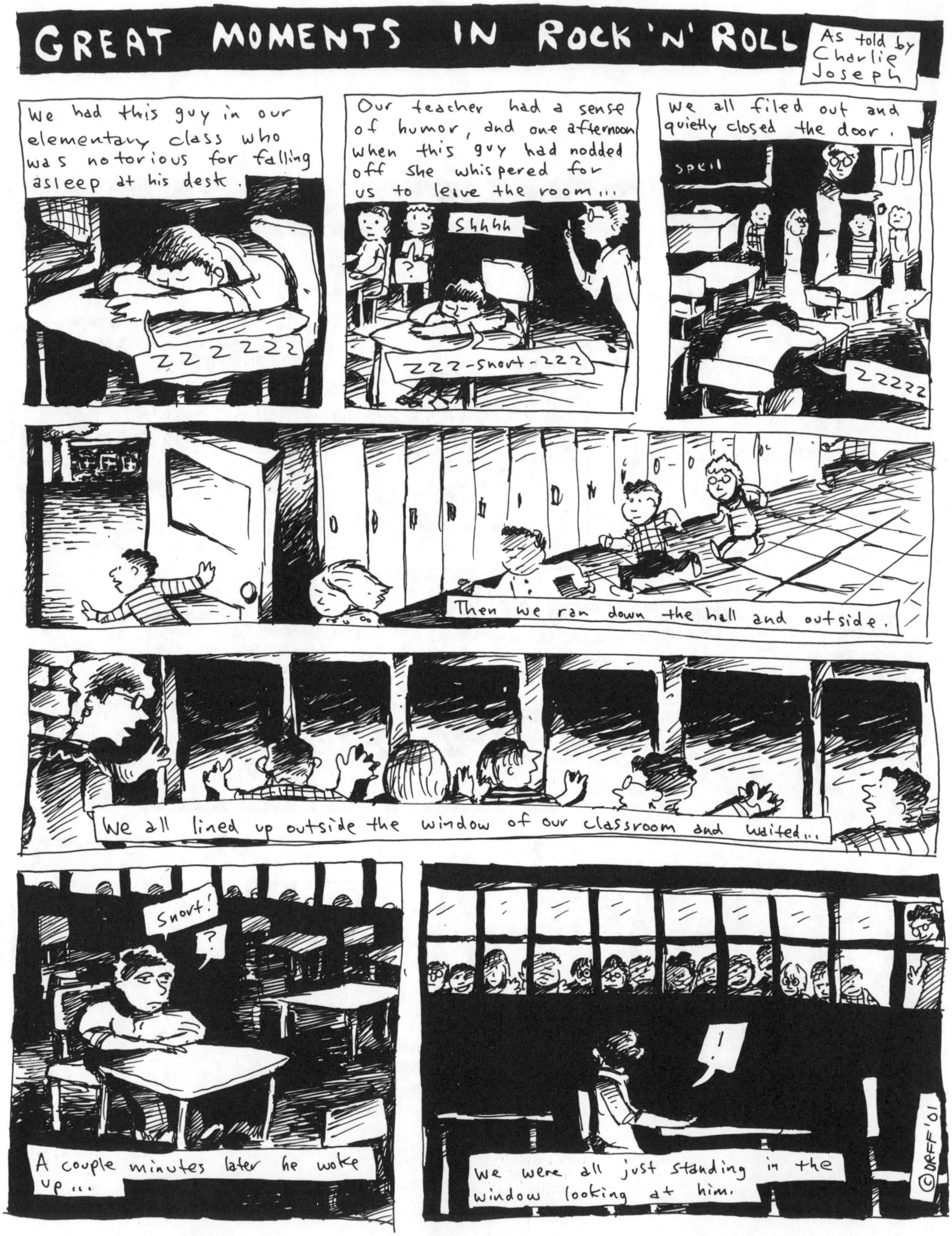
GREAT MOMENTS IN ROCK 'N' ROLL
As told by Charlie Joseph
We had this guy in our elementary class who was notorious for falling asleep at his desk.
ZZZZZZ
Our teacher had a sense of humor, and one afternoon when this guy had nodded off she whispered for us to leave the room...
Shhhh
?
ZZZ-snort-ZZZ
We all filed out and quietly closed the door.
ZZZZZ
Then we ran down the hall and outside.
We all lined up outside the window of our classroom and waited...
Snort!
?
A couple minutes later he woke up...
!
We were all just standing in the window looking at him.
©DREFF '01

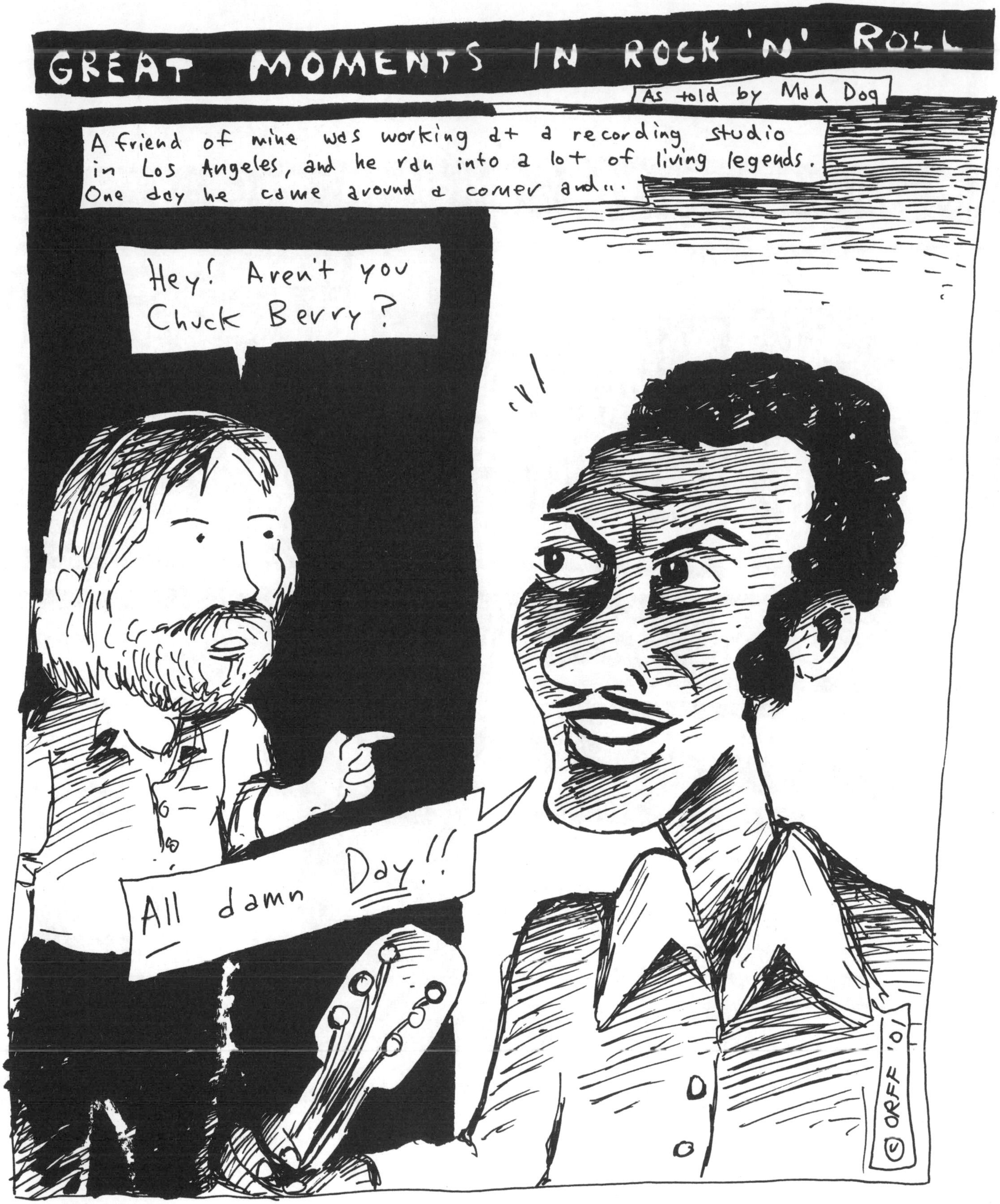
GREAT MOMENTS IN ROCK 'N' ROLL
As told by Mad Dog
A friend of mine was working at a recording studio in Los Angeles, and he ran into a lot of living legends. One day he came around a corner and...
Hey! Aren't you Chuck Berry?
All damn Day!!
© ORFF '01

GREAT MOMENTS IN ROCK 'N' ROLL

As told by Maaaaac

It was our first date. My first date. I picked her up at her folks!

I wanted everything to go right.

We were going out to see a movie. Funny, I can't even remember what it was now.

Maybe that's because we almost didn't get to see it...

When we got there the film was sold out.

We got tickets for the later show, but now we had two hours to kill.

Things had been going so well. I had to come up with something else to do to keep the good times rolling...

We got back in the car and started driving around.

I finally hit on what I thought was the perfect solution.

screeeooo

I cranked up the radio and drove out onto White Bear Lake, where we whipped fishhooks for about an hour.

She didn't really get into it.

FA! I feel for you Chaka-Khan ♪

Wooooooooo!

By the time I dropped her off, I knew that this would be our last date.

I still think that fishhooks rock.

© ORFF '00

34

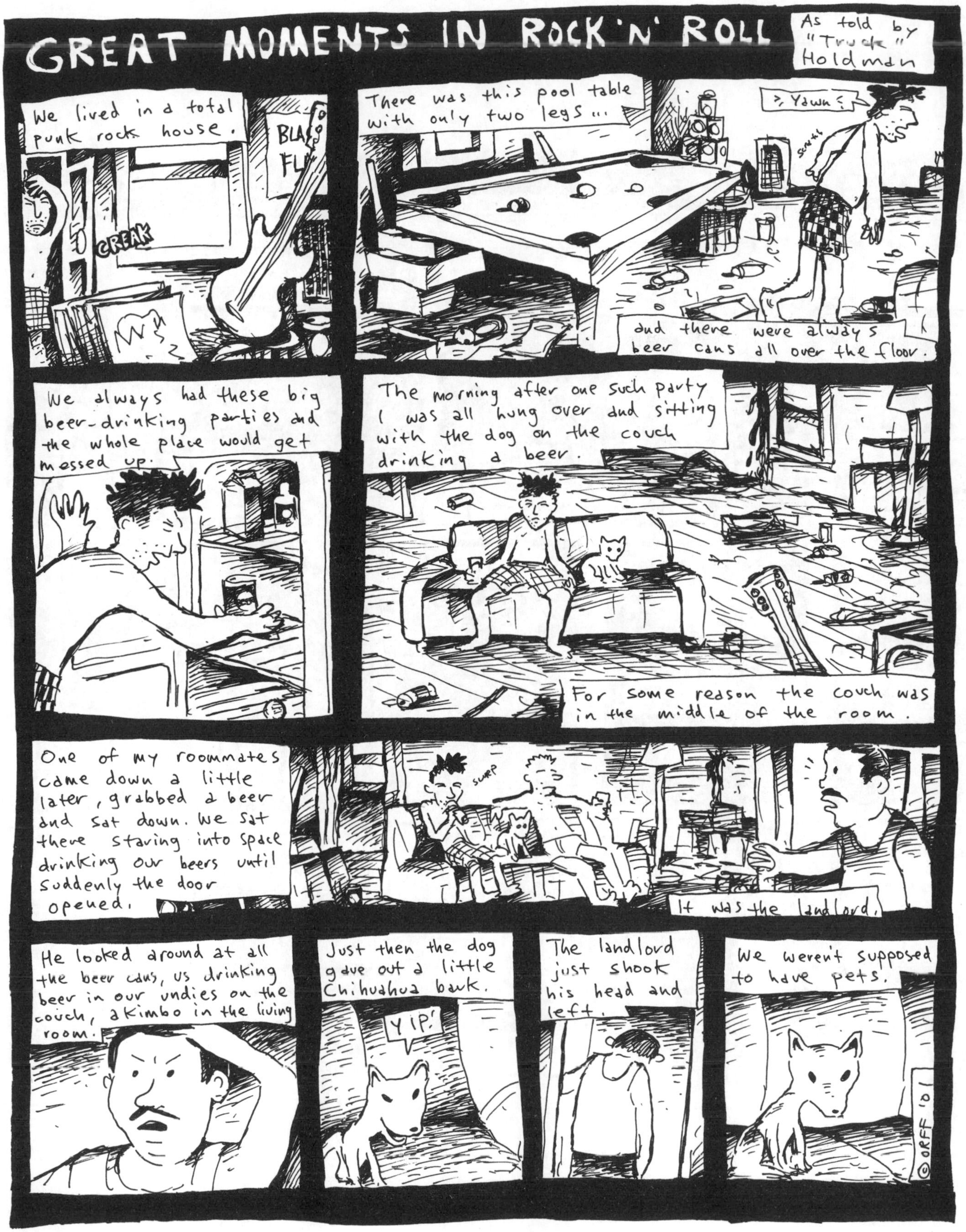

GREAT MOMENTS IN ROCK 'N' ROLL
As told by "Truck" Holdman
We lived in a total punk rock house.
CREAK
There was this pool table with only two legs...
> Yawn <
and there were always beer cans all over the floor.
We always had these big beer-drinking parties and the whole place would get messed up.
The morning after one such party I was all hung over and sitting with the dog on the couch drinking a beer.
For some reason the couch was in the middle of the room.
One of my roommates came down a little later, grabbed a beer and sat down. We sat there staring into space drinking our beers until suddenly the door opened.
SLURP
It was the landlord.
He looked around at all the beer cans, us drinking beer in our undies on the couch, akimbo in the living room.
Just then the dog gave out a little Chihuahua bark.
YIP!
The landlord just shook his head and left.
We weren't supposed to have pets.
©ORFF '01

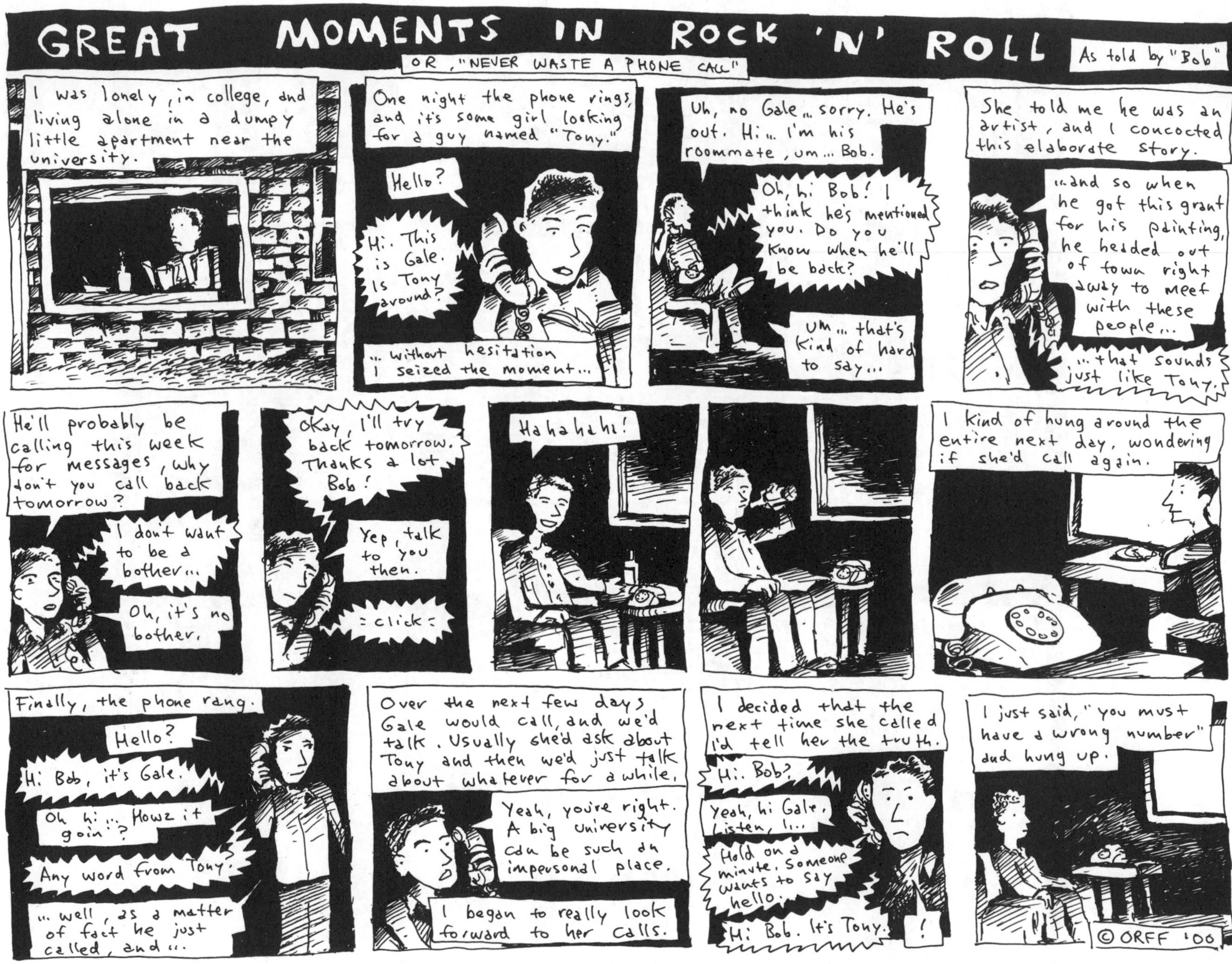
GREAT MOMENTS IN ROCK 'N' ROLL
OR, "NEVER WASTE A PHONE CALL"
As told by "Bob"
I was lonely, in college, and living alone in a dumpy little apartment near the university.
One night the phone rings, and it's some girl looking for a guy named "Tony."
Hello?
Hi. This is Gale. Is Tony around?
...without hesitation I seized the moment...
Uh, no Gale... sorry. He's out. Hi... I'm his roommate, um... Bob.
Oh, hi Bob! I think he's mentioned you. Do you know when he'll be back?
Um... that's kind of hard to say...
She told me he was an artist, and I concocted this elaborate story.
...and so when he got this grant for his painting, he headed out of town right away to meet with these people...
...that sounds just like Tony.
He'll probably be calling this week for messages, why don't you call back tomorrow?
I don't want to be a bother...
Oh, it's no bother.
Okay, I'll try back tomorrow. Thanks a lot Bob!
Yep, talk to you then.
=click=
Hahahaha!
I kind of hung around the entire next day, wondering if she'd call again.
Finally, the phone rang.
Hello?
Hi Bob, it's Gale.
Oh hi... Howz it goin'?
Any word from Tony?
...well, as a matter of fact he just called, and...
Over the next few days Gale would call, and we'd talk. Usually she'd ask about Tony and then we'd just talk about whatever for a while.
Yeah, you're right. A big university can be such an impersonal place.
I began to really look forward to her calls.
I decided that the next time she called I'd tell her the truth.
Hi. Bob?
Yeah, hi Gale. Listen, I...
Hold on a minute. Someone wants to say hello.
Hi Bob. It's Tony.
!
I just said, "you must have a wrong number" and hung up.
© ORFF '00

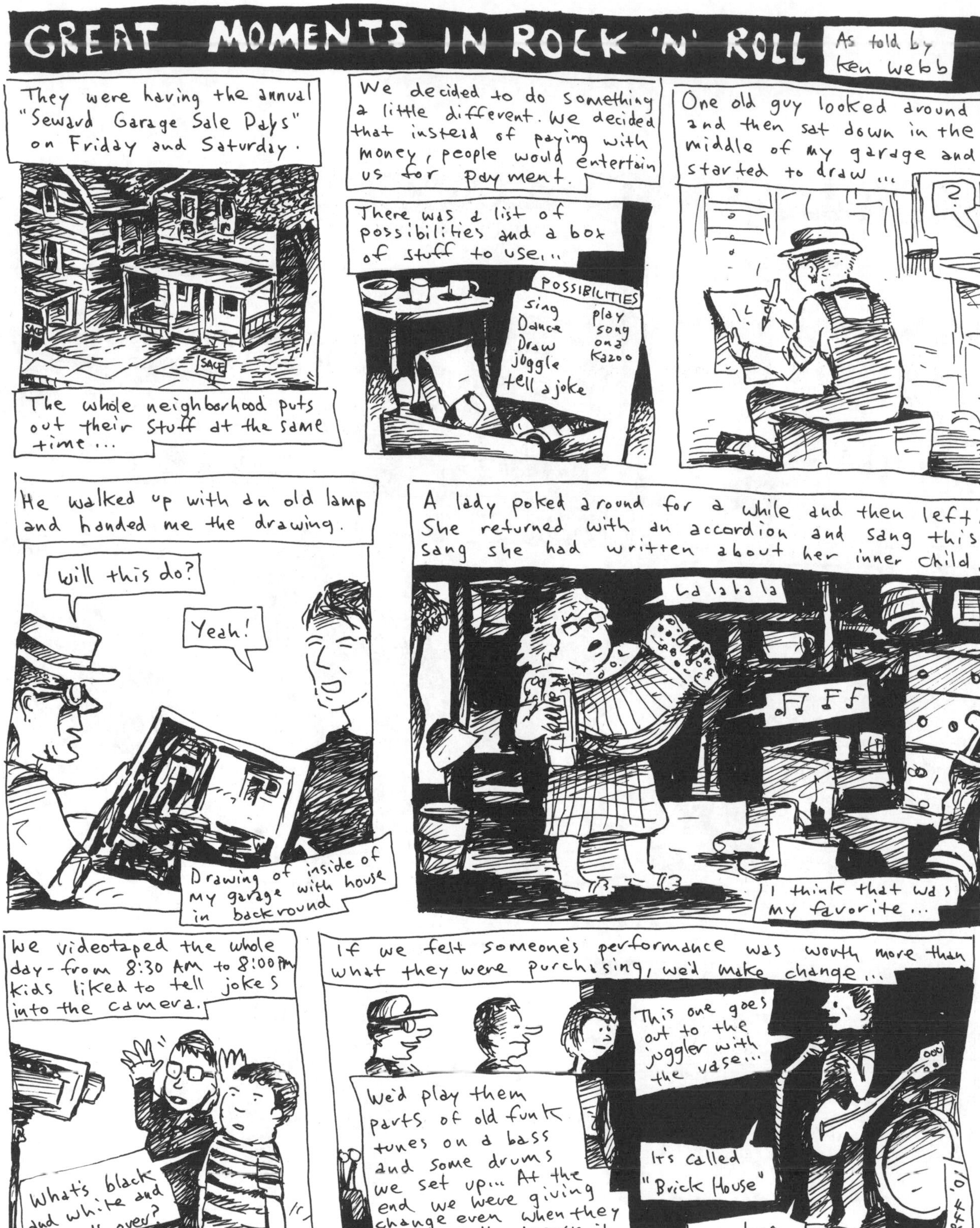
GREAT MOMENTS IN ROCK 'N' ROLL
As told by Ken Webb
They were having the annual "Seward Garage Sale Days" on Friday and Saturday.
SALE
SALE
The whole neighborhood puts out their Stuff at the same time...
We decided to do something a little different. We decided that instead of paying with money, people would entertain us for payment.
There was a list of possibilities and a box of stuff to use...
POSSIBILITIES
sing
Dance
Draw
juggle
tell a joke
play song on a Kazoo
One old guy looked around and then sat down in the middle of my garage and started to draw...
?
He walked up with an old lamp and handed me the drawing.
Will this do?
Yeah!
Drawing of inside of my garage with house in backround
A lady poked around for a while and then left. She returned with an accordion and sang this song she had written about her inner child.
La la la la la
I think that was my favorite...
We videotaped the whole day - from 8:30 AM to 8:00 PM
Kids liked to tell jokes into the camera.
What's black and white and read all over?
If we felt someone's performance was worth more than what they were purchasing, we'd make change...
We'd play them parts of old funk tunes on a bass and some drums we set up... At the end we were giving change even when they didn't really deserve it. Partly to get people to go home.
This one goes out to the juggler with the vase...
It's called "Brick House"
one two THREE!
© ORFF '01

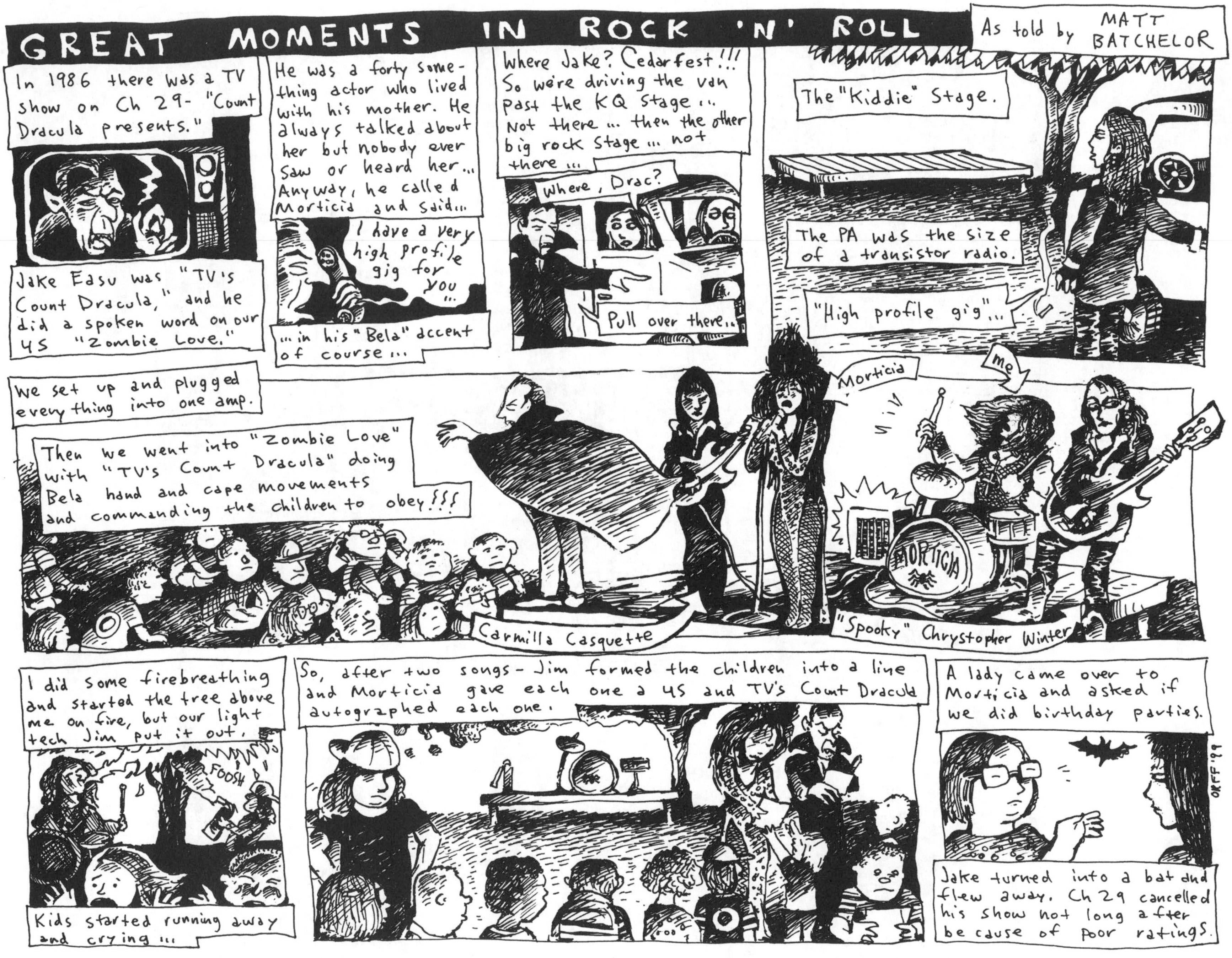
GREAT MOMENTS IN ROCK 'N' ROLL
As told by MATT BATCHELOR
In 1986 there was a TV show on Ch 29- "Count Dracula presents."
Jake Easu was "TV's Count Dracula," and he did a spoken word on our 45 "Zombie Love."
He was a forty something actor who lived with his mother. He always talked about her but nobody ever saw or heard her... Anyway, he called Morticia and said...
I have a very high profile gig for you...
... in his "Bela" accent of course...
Where Jake? Cedarfest!!! So we're driving the van past the KQ stage... Not there... then the other big rock stage... not there...
Where, Drac?
Pull over there..
The "Kiddie" Stage.
The PA was the size of a transistor radio.
"High profile gig"...
We set up and plugged everything into one amp.
Then we went into "Zombie Love" with "TV's Count Dracula" doing Bela hand and cape movements and commanding the children to obey!!!
Morticia
me
MORTICIA
Carmilla Casquette
"Spooky" Chrystopher Winter
I did some firebreathing and started the tree above me on fire, but our light tech Jim put it out.
FOOSH
Kids started running away and crying...
So, after two songs - Jim formed the children into a line and Morticia gave each one a 45 and TV's Count Dracula autographed each one.
A lady came over to Morticia and asked if we did birthday parties.
Jake turned into a bat and flew away. Ch 29 cancelled his show not long after because of poor ratings.
ORFF '99

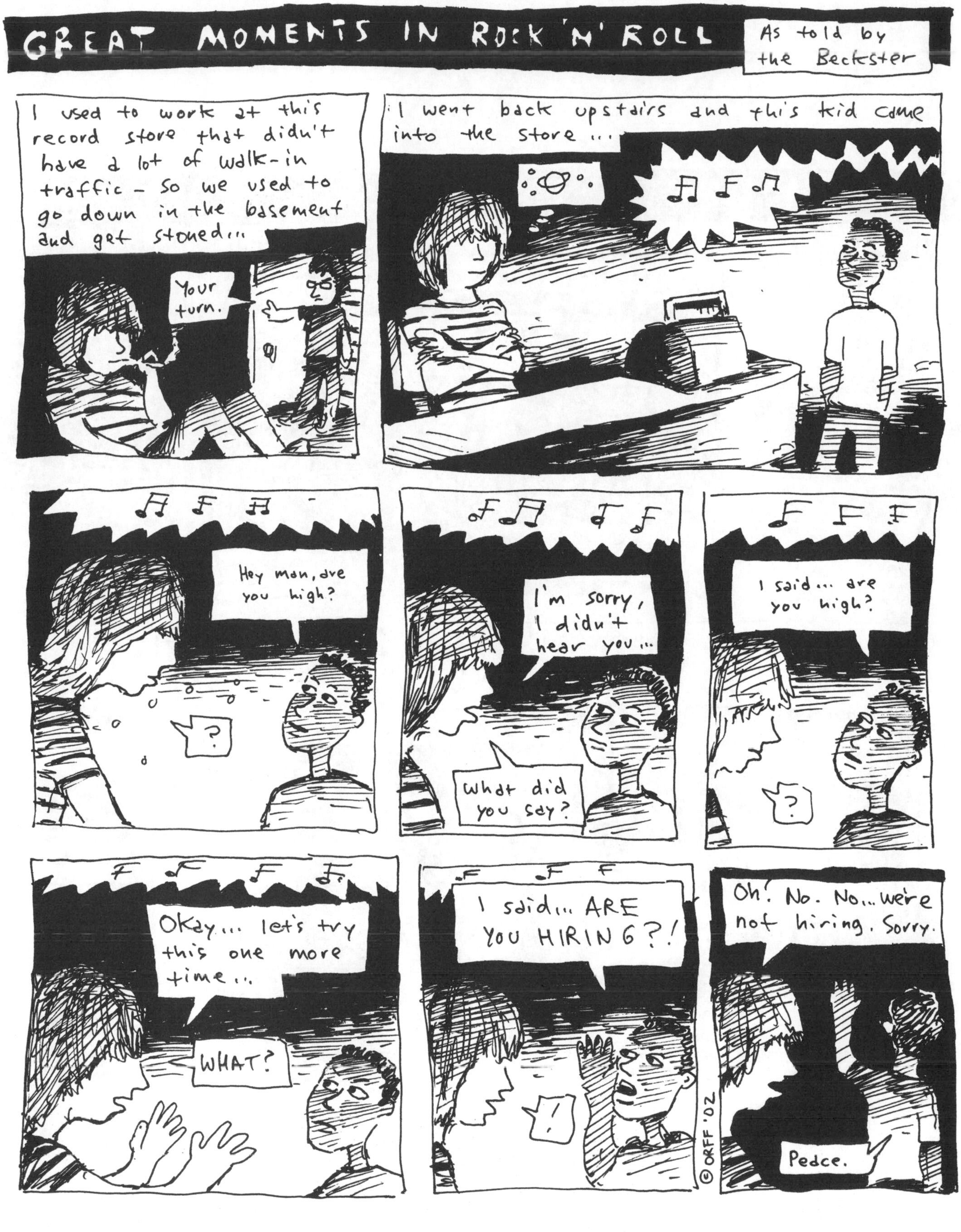
GREAT MOMENTS IN ROCK 'N' ROLL
As told by the Beckster
I used to work at this record store that didn't have a lot of walk-in traffic - so we used to go down in the basement and get stoned...
Your turn.
I went back upstairs and this kid came into the store...
Hey man, are you high?
?
I'm sorry, I didn't hear you...
What did you say?
I said... are you high?
?
Okay... let's try this one more time...
WHAT?
I said... ARE YOU HIRING?!
!
© ORFF '02
Oh! No. No... we're not hiring. Sorry.
Peace.

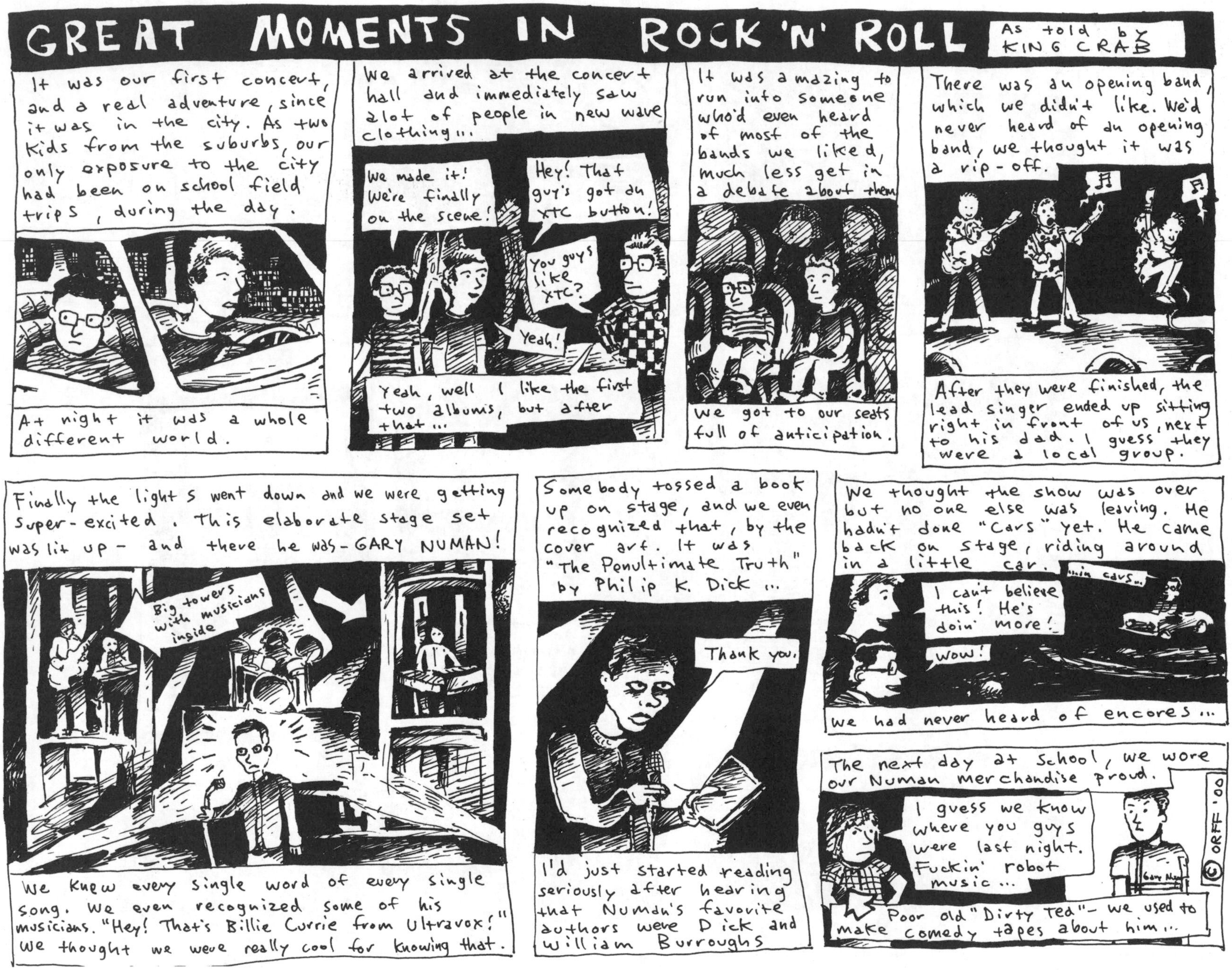
GREAT MOMENTS IN ROCK 'N' ROLL
As told by KING CRAB
It was our first concert, and a real adventure, since it was in the city. As two kids from the suburbs, our only exposure to the city had been on school field trips, during the day.
At night it was a whole different world.
We arrived at the concert hall and immediately saw alot of people in new wave clothing...
We made it! We're finally on the scene!
Hey! That guy's got an XTC button!
You guys like XTC?
Yeah!
Yeah, well I like the first two albums, but after that...
It was amazing to run into someone who'd even heard of most of the bands we liked, much less get in a debate about them
We got to our seats full of anticipation.
There was an opening band, which we didn't like. We'd never heard of an opening band, we thought it was a rip-off.
After they were finished, the lead singer ended up sitting right in front of us, next to his dad. I guess they were a local group.
Finally the lights went down and we were getting super-excited. This elaborate stage set was lit up - and there he was - GARY NUMAN!
Big towers with musicians inside
We knew every single word of every single song. We even recognized some of his musicians. "Hey! That's Billie Currie from Ultravox!" We thought we were really cool for knowing that.
Somebody tossed a book up on stage, and we even recognized that, by the cover art. It was "The Penultimate Truth" by Philip K. Dick...
Thank you.
I'd just started reading seriously after hearing that Numan's favorite authors were Dick and William Burroughs
We thought the show was over but no one else was leaving. He hadn't done "Cars" yet. He came back on stage, riding around in a little car.
...in cars...
I can't believe this! He's doin' more!
Wow!
We had never heard of encores...
The next day at school, we wore our Numan merchandise proud.
I guess we know where you guys were last night. Fuckin' robot music...
Poor old "Dirty Ted" - we used to make comedy tapes about him...
© ORFF '00

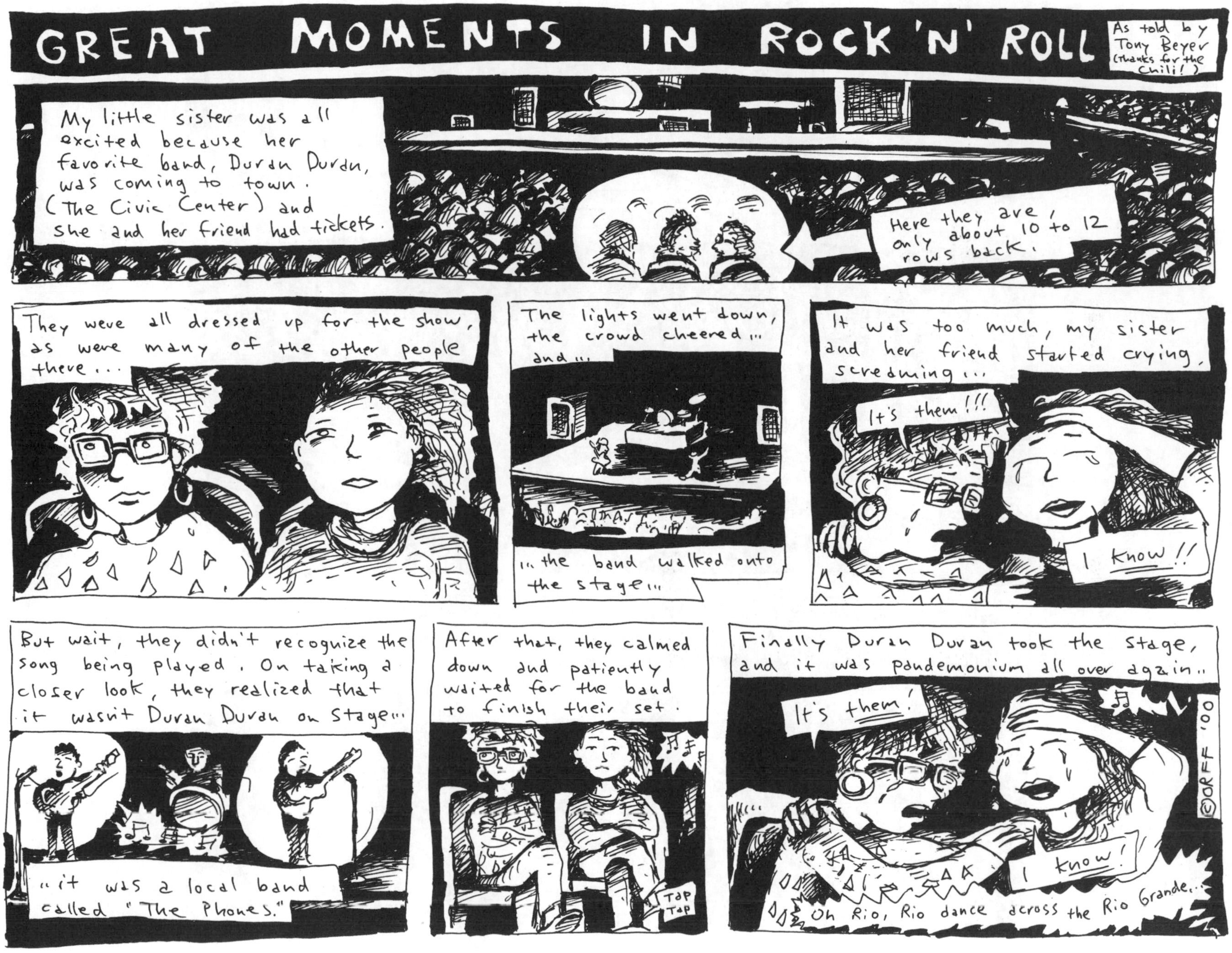
GREAT MOMENTS IN ROCK 'N' ROLL
As told by Tony Beyer (thanks for the chili!)
My little sister was all excited because her favorite band, Duran Duran, was coming to town. (The Civic Center) and she and her friend had tickets.
Here they are, only about 10 to 12 rows back.
They were all dressed up for the show, as were many of the other people there...
The lights went down, the crowd cheered... and...
...the band walked onto the stage...
It was too much, my sister and her friend started crying, screaming...
It's them!!!
I know!!
But wait, they didn't recognize the song being played. On taking a closer look, they realized that it wasn't Duran Duran on stage...
...it was a local band called "The Phones."
After that, they calmed down and patiently waited for the band to finish their set.
Tap Tap
Finally Duran Duran took the stage, and it was pandemonium all over again...
It's them!
I know!
Oh Rio, Rio dance across the Rio Grande...
©ORFF '00

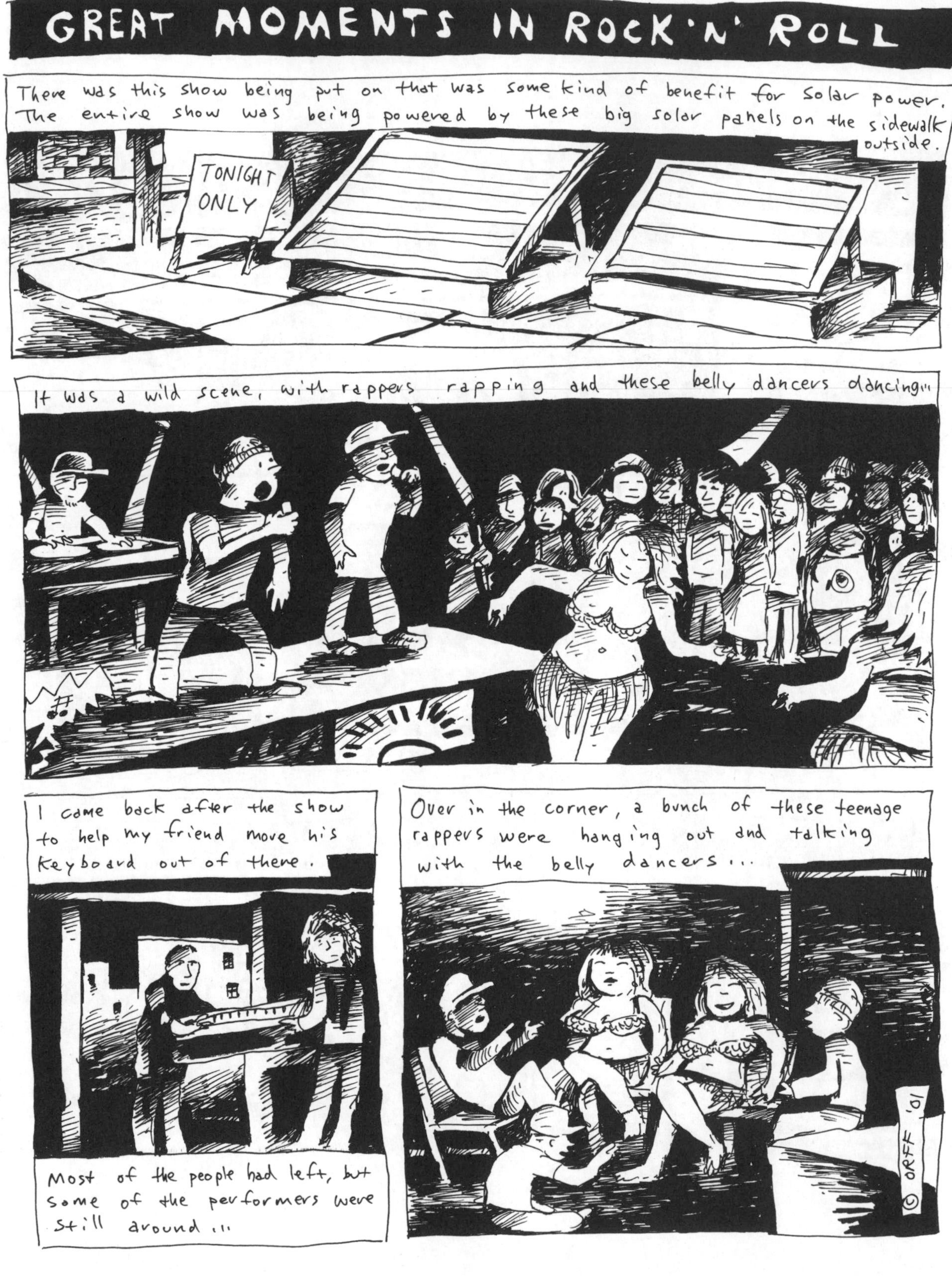
GREAT MOMENTS IN ROCK 'N' ROLL
There was this show being put on that was some kind of benefit for solar power. The entire show was being powered by these big solar panels on the sidewalk outside.
TONIGHT ONLY
It was a wild scene, with rappers rapping and these belly dancers dancing...
I came back after the show to help my friend move his keyboard out of there.
Most of the people had left, but some of the performers were still around...
Over in the corner, a bunch of these teenage rappers were hanging out and talking with the belly dancers...
© ORFF '01

GREAT MOMENTS IN ROCK 'N' ROLL

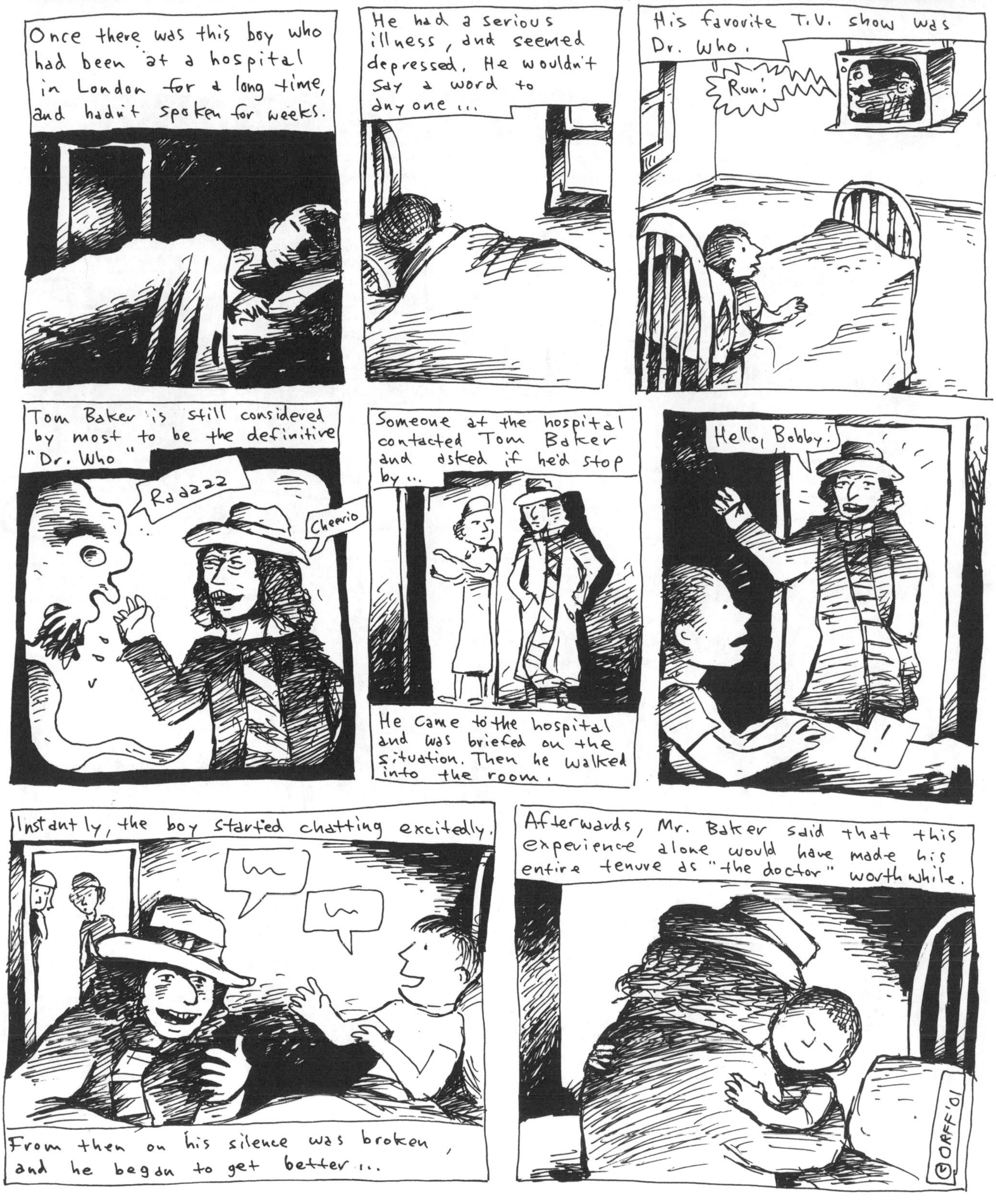
Once there was this boy who had been at a hospital in London for a long time, and hadn't spoken for weeks.
He had a serious illness, and seemed depressed. He wouldn't say a word to anyone...
His favorite T.V. show was Dr. Who.
Run!
Tom Baker is still considered by most to be the definitive "Dr. Who"
Radazz
Cheerio
Someone at the hospital contacted Tom Baker and asked if he'd stop by...
He came to the hospital and was briefed on the situation. Then he walked into the room.
Hello, Bobby!
!
Instantly, the boy started chatting excitedly.
From then on his silence was broken, and he began to get better...
Afterwards, Mr. Baker said that this experience alone would have made his entire tenure as "the doctor" worthwhile.
© ORFF '01

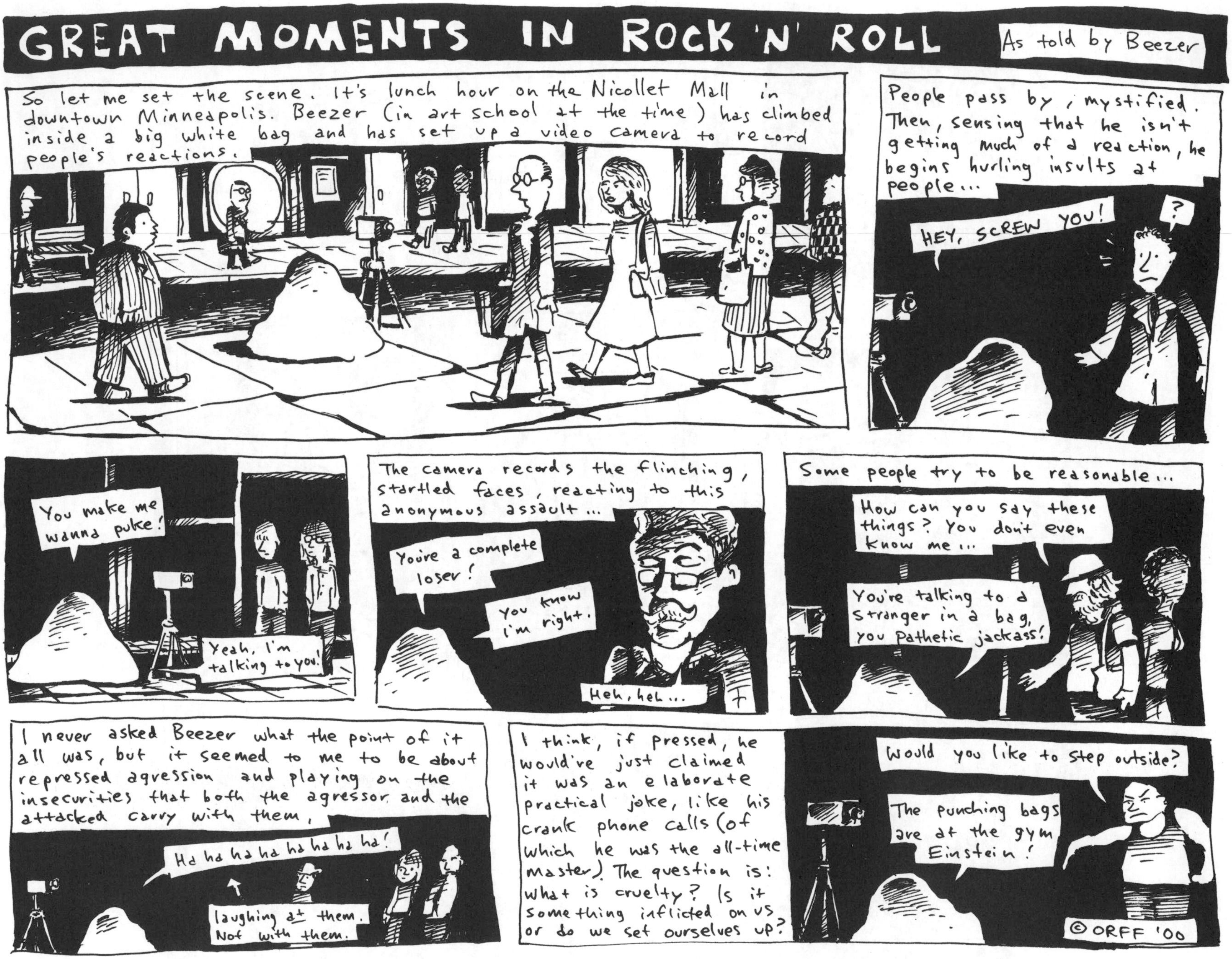
GREAT MOMENTS IN ROCK 'N' ROLL
As told by Beezer
So let me set the scene. It's lunch hour on the Nicollet Mall in downtown Minneapolis. Beezer (in art school at the time) has climbed inside a big white bag and has set up a video camera to record people's reactions.
People pass by, mystified. Then, sensing that he isn't getting much of a reaction, he begins hurling insults at people...
HEY, SCREW YOU!
?
You make me wanna puke!
Yeah, I'm talking to you!
The camera records the flinching, startled faces, reacting to this anonymous assault...
You're a complete loser!
You know I'm right.
Heh, heh...
Some people try to be reasonable...
How can you say these things? You don't even know me...
You're talking to a stranger in a bag, you pathetic jackass!
I never asked Beezer what the point of it all was, but it seemed to me to be about repressed agression and playing on the insecurities that both the agressor and the attacked carry with them,
Ha ha ha ha ha ha ha ha!
laughing at them. Not with them.
I think, if pressed, he would've just claimed it was an elaborate practical joke, like his crank phone calls (of which he was the all-time master) The question is: what is cruelty? Is it something inflicted on us or do we set ourselves up?
Would you like to step outside?
The punching bags are at the gym Einstein!
© ORFF '00

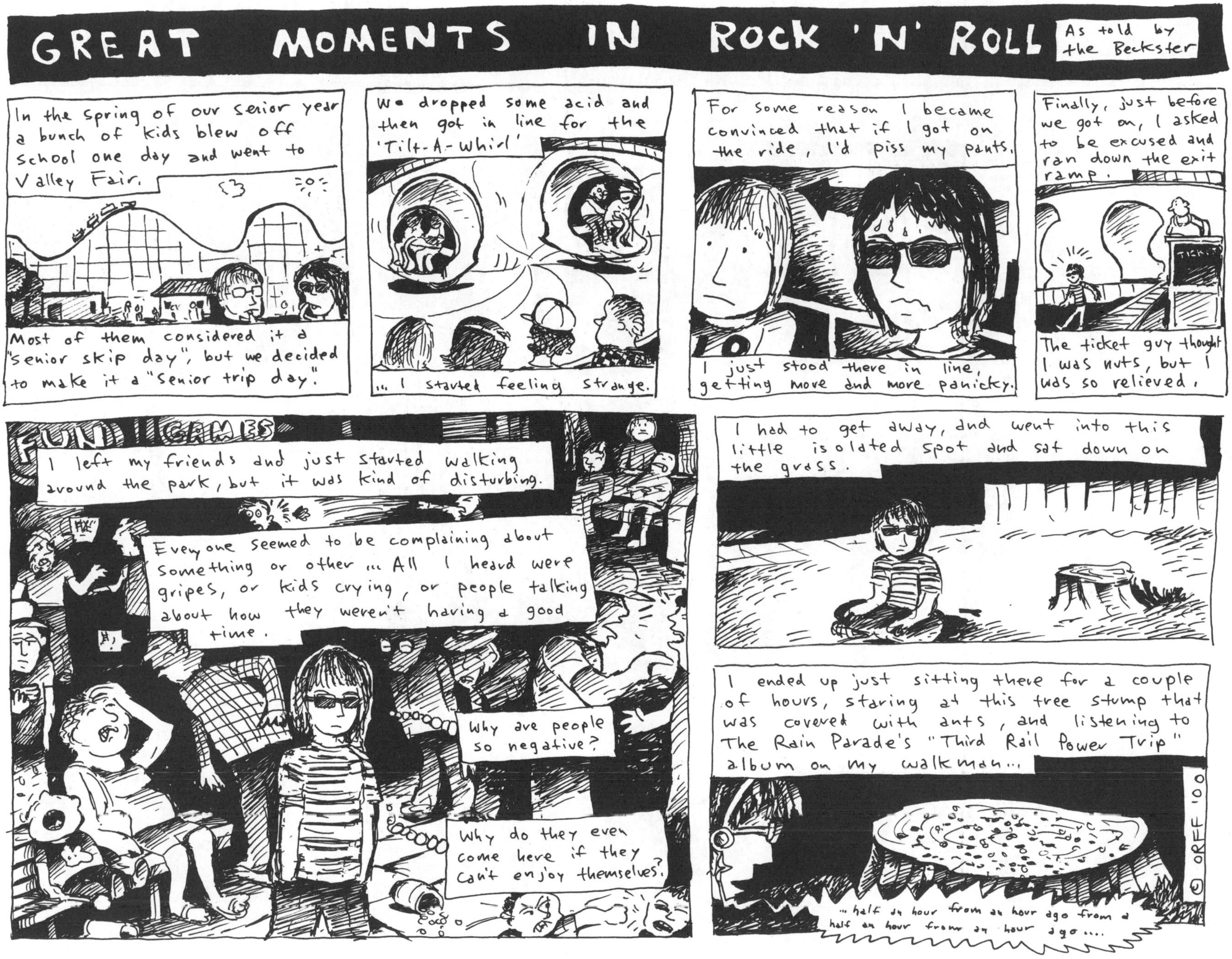
GREAT MOMENTS IN ROCK 'N' ROLL
As told by the Beckster
In the spring of our senior year a bunch of kids blew off school one day and went to Valley Fair.
Most of them considered it a "senior skip day", but we decided to make it a "senior trip day."
We dropped some acid and then got in line for the 'Tilt-A-Whirl'
... I started feeling strange.
For some reason I became convinced that if I got on the ride, I'd piss my pants.
I just stood there in line, getting more and more panicky.
Finally, just before we got on, I asked to be excused and ran down the exit ramp.
The ticket guy thought I was nuts, but I was so relieved.
FUN GAMES
I left my friends and just started walking around the park, but it was kind of disturbing.
Everyone seemed to be complaining about something or other ... All I heard were gripes, or kids crying, or people talking about how they weren't having a good time.
Why are people so negative?
Why do they even come here if they can't enjoy themselves?
I had to get away, and went into this little isolated spot and sat down on the grass.
I ended up just sitting there for a couple of hours, staring at this tree stump that was covered with ants, and listening to The Rain Parade's "Third Rail Power Trip" album on my walkman...
... half an hour from an hour ago from a half an hour from an hour ago....
© ORFF '00

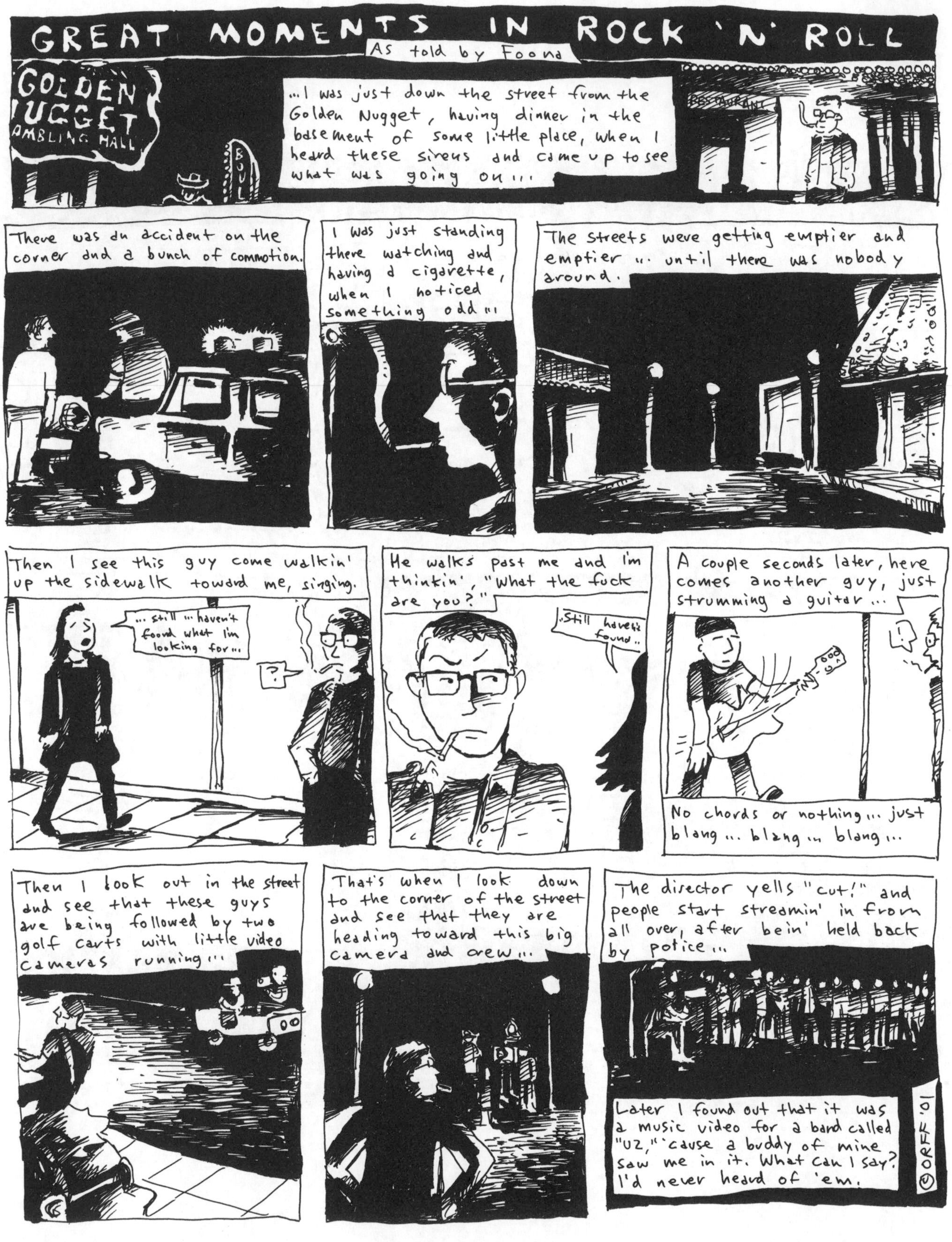
GREAT MOMENTS IN ROCK 'N' ROLL
As told by Foona
GOLDEN NUGGET GAMBLING HALL
...I was just down the street from the Golden Nugget, having dinner in the basement of some little place, when I heard these sirens and came up to see what was going on...
RESTAURANT
There was an accident on the corner and a bunch of commotion.
I was just standing there watching and having a cigarette, when I noticed something odd...
The streets were getting emptier and emptier... until there was nobody around.
Then I see this guy come walkin' up the sidewalk toward me, singing.
...still... haven't found what I'm looking for...
?
He walks past me and I'm thinkin', "What the fuck are you?"
Still haven't found..
A couple seconds later, here comes another guy, just strumming a guitar...
!
No chords or nothing... just blang... blang... blang...
Then I look out in the street and see that these guys are being followed by two golf carts with little video cameras running...
That's when I look down to the corner of the street and see that they are heading toward this big camera and crew...
The director yells "cut!" and people start streamin' in from all over, after bein' held back by police...
Later I found out that it was a music video for a band called "U2," 'cause a buddy of mine saw me in it. What can I say? I'd never heard of 'em.
©ORFF '01

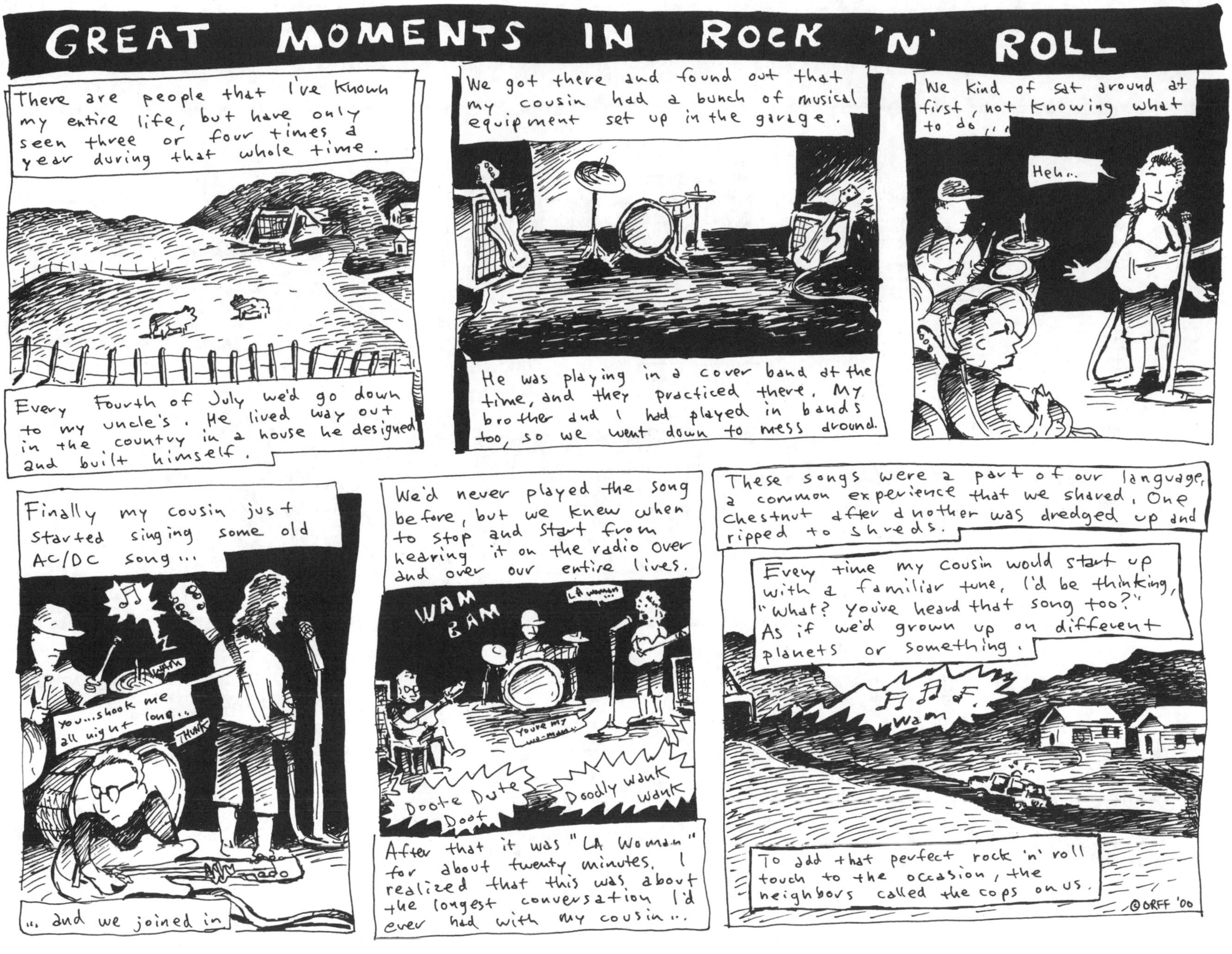
GREAT MOMENTS IN ROCK 'N' ROLL
There are people that I've known my entire life, but have only seen three or four times a year during that whole time.
Every Fourth of July we'd go down to my uncle's. He lived way out in the country in a house he designed and built himself.
We got there and found out that my cousin had a bunch of musical equipment set up in the garage.
He was playing in a cover band at the time, and they practiced there. My brother and I had played in bands too, so we went down to mess around.
We kind of sat around at first, not knowing what to do...
Heh..
Finally my cousin just started singing some old AC/DC song...
You...shook me all night long..
THUNK
.. and we joined in.
We'd never played the song before, but we knew when to stop and start from hearing it on the radio over and over our entire lives.
WAM BAM
You're my wo-man...
Doote Dute Doot
Doodly wank wank
After that it was "LA Woman" for about twenty minutes. I realized that this was about the longest conversation I'd ever had with my cousin..
These songs were a part of our language, a common experience that we shared. One chestnut after another was dredged up and ripped to shreds.
Every time my cousin would start up with a familiar tune, I'd be thinking, "What? You've heard that song too?" As if we'd grown up on different planets or something.
Wam
To add that perfect rock 'n' roll touch to the occasion, the neighbors called the cops on us.
©ORFF '00

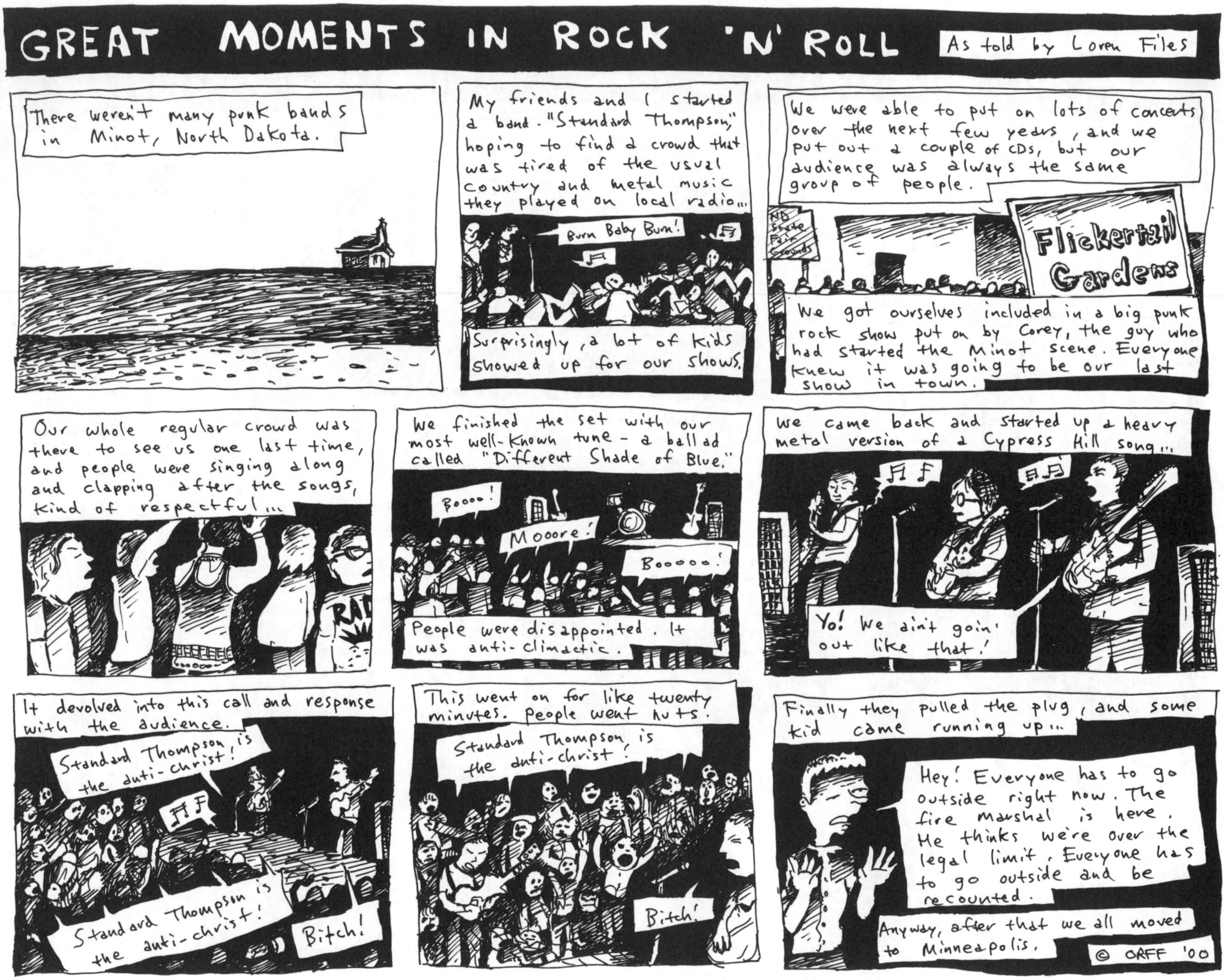
GREAT MOMENTS IN ROCK 'N' ROLL
As told by Loren Files
There weren't many punk bands in Minot, North Dakota.
My friends and I started a band - "Standard Thompson," hoping to find a crowd that was tired of the usual country and metal music they played on local radio...
Burn Baby Burn!
Surprisingly, a lot of kids showed up for our shows.
We were able to put on lots of concerts over the next few years, and we put out a couple of CDs, but our audience was always the same group of people.
ND State Fair Grounds
Flickertail Gardens
We got ourselves included in a big punk rock show put on by Corey, the guy who had started the Minot scene. Everyone knew it was going to be our last show in town.
Our whole regular crowd was there to see us one last time, and people were singing along and clapping after the songs, kind of respectful...
RAD
We finished the set with our most well-known tune - a ballad called "Different Shade of Blue."
Boooo!
Mooore!
Booooo!
People were disappointed. It was anti-climactic.
We came back and started up a heavy metal version of a Cypress Hill song...
Yo! We ain't goin' out like that!
It devolved into this call and response with the audience.
Standard Thompson is the anti-christ!
Standard Thompson is the anti-christ!
Bitch!
This went on for like twenty minutes. People went nuts.
Standard Thompson is the anti-christ!
Bitch!
Finally they pulled the plug, and some kid came running up...
Hey! Everyone has to go outside right now. The fire marshal is here. He thinks we're over the legal limit. Everyone has to go outside and be recounted.
Anyway, after that we all moved to Minneapolis.
© ORFF '00

GREAT MOMENTS IN ROCK 'N' ROLL
So, how was your day?
Oh, it went slick as snot. We got out of bed...
Ka-ching
...went downtown...
Tibbla bomp bomp
Caught the bus..
Shikka shikka eeert!
Made it across town..
Schwabang
Cruised into the stadium..
CHHHCHHH
Cut that out.
Anyway, it was a great game.
Cool.
Right?
?
© ORFF '01

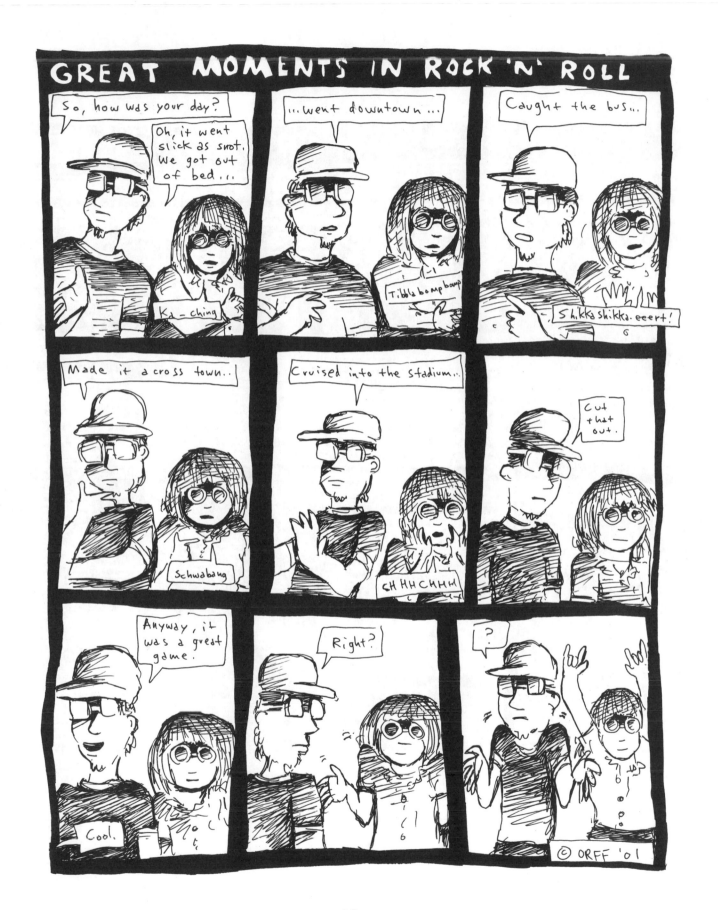

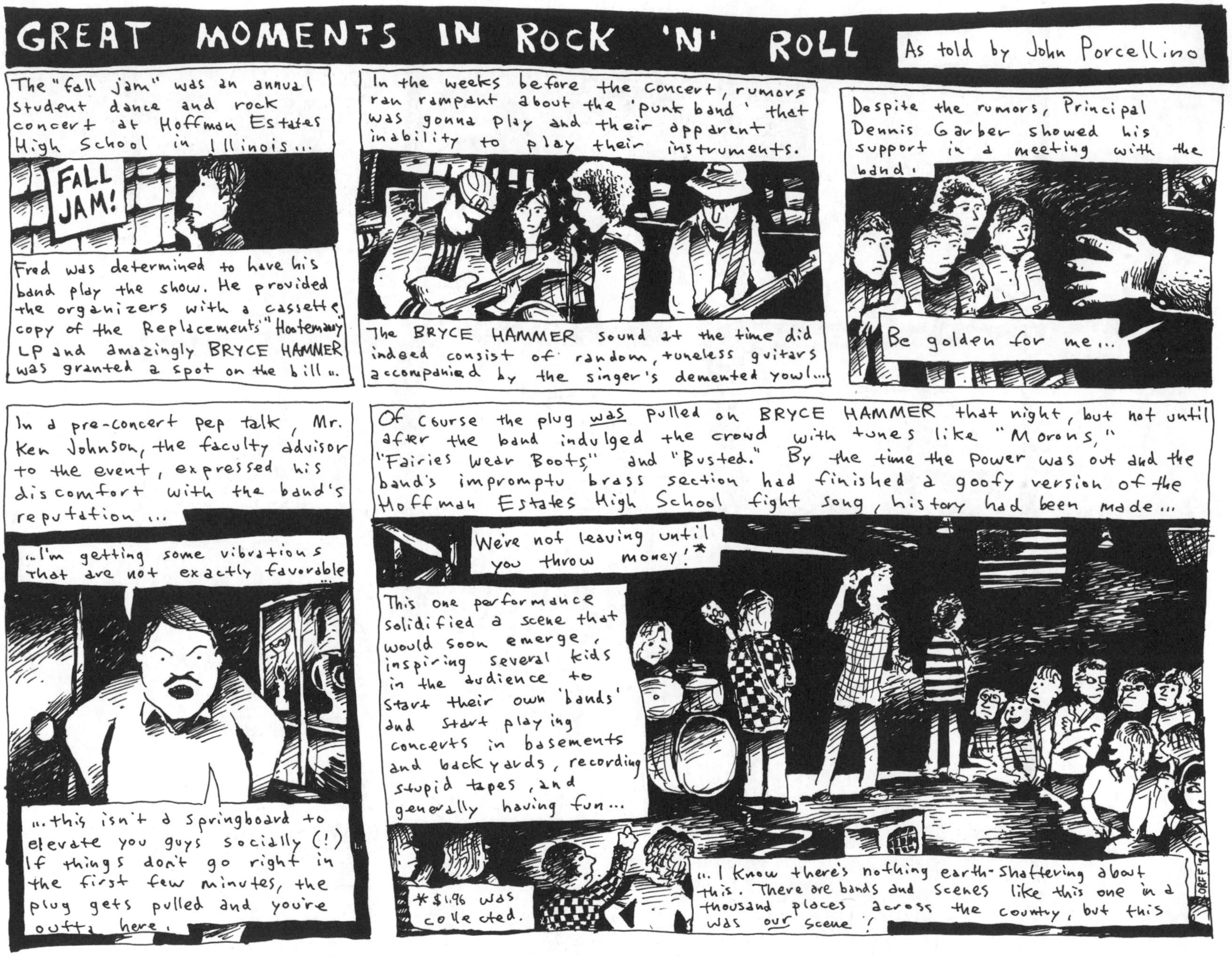
GREAT MOMENTS IN ROCK 'N' ROLL
As told by John Porcellino
The "fall jam" was an annual student dance and rock concert at Hoffman Estates High School in Illinois...
FALL JAM!
Fred was determined to have his band play the show. He provided the organizers with a cassette copy of the Replacements' "Hootenanny" LP and amazingly BRYCE HAMMER was granted a spot on the bill...
In the weeks before the concert, rumors ran rampant about the 'punk band' that was gonna play and their apparent inability to play their instruments.
The BRYCE HAMMER sound at the time did indeed consist of random, tuneless guitars accompanied by the singer's demented yowl...
Despite the rumors, Principal Dennis Garber showed his support in a meeting with the band.
Be golden for me...
In a pre-concert pep talk, Mr. Ken Johnson, the faculty advisor to the event, expressed his discomfort with the band's reputation...
...I'm getting some vibrations that are not exactly favorable...
...this isn't a springboard to elevate you guys socially (!) If things don't go right in the first few minutes, the plug gets pulled and you're outta here.
Of course the plug was pulled on BRYCE HAMMER that night, but not until after the band indulged the crowd with tunes like "Morons," "Fairies Wear Boots" and "Busted." By the time the power was out and the band's impromptu brass section had finished a goofy version of the Hoffman Estates High School fight song, history had been made...
We're not leaving until you throw money!*
This one performance solidified a scene that would soon emerge, inspiring several kids in the audience to start their own 'bands' and start playing concerts in basements and backyards, recording stupid tapes, and generally having fun...
*$1.96 was collected.
...I know there's nothing earth-shattering about this. There are bands and scenes like this one in a thousand places across the country, but this was our scene!

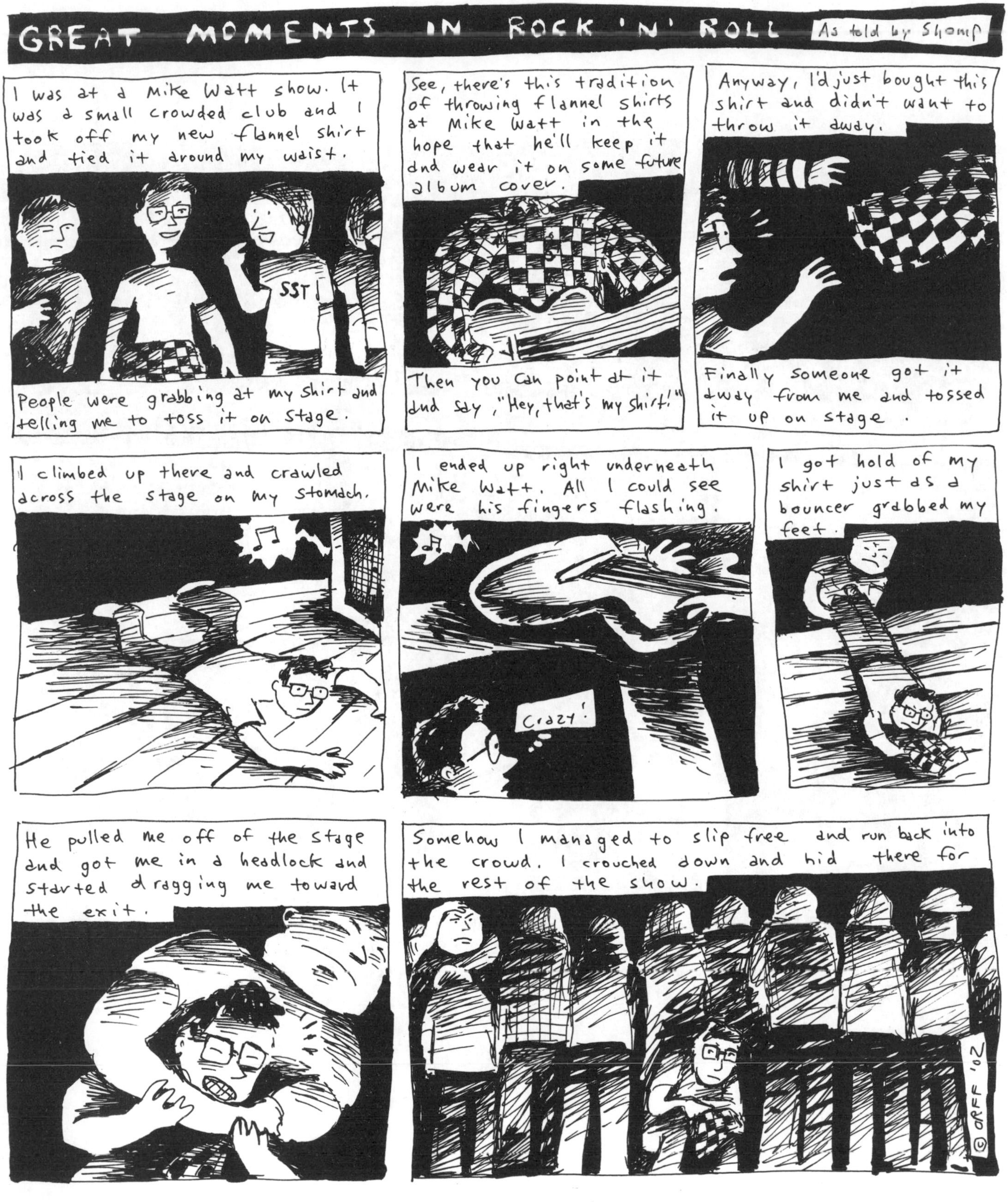
GREAT MOMENTS IN ROCK 'N' ROLL
As told by Shomp
I was at a Mike Watt show. It was a small crowded club and I took off my new flannel shirt and tied it around my waist.
SST
People were grabbing at my shirt and telling me to toss it on stage.
See, there's this tradition of throwing flannel shirts at Mike Watt in the hope that he'll keep it and wear it on some future album cover.
Then you can point at it and say, "Hey, that's my shirt!"
Anyway, I'd just bought this shirt and didn't want to throw it away.
Finally someone got it away from me and tossed it up on stage.
I climbed up there and crawled across the stage on my stomach.
I ended up right underneath Mike Watt. All I could see were his fingers flashing.
Crazy!
I got hold of my shirt just as a bouncer grabbed my feet.
He pulled me off of the stage and got me in a headlock and started dragging me toward the exit.
Somehow I managed to slip free and run back into the crowd. I crouched down and hid there for the rest of the show.
© ORFF '02

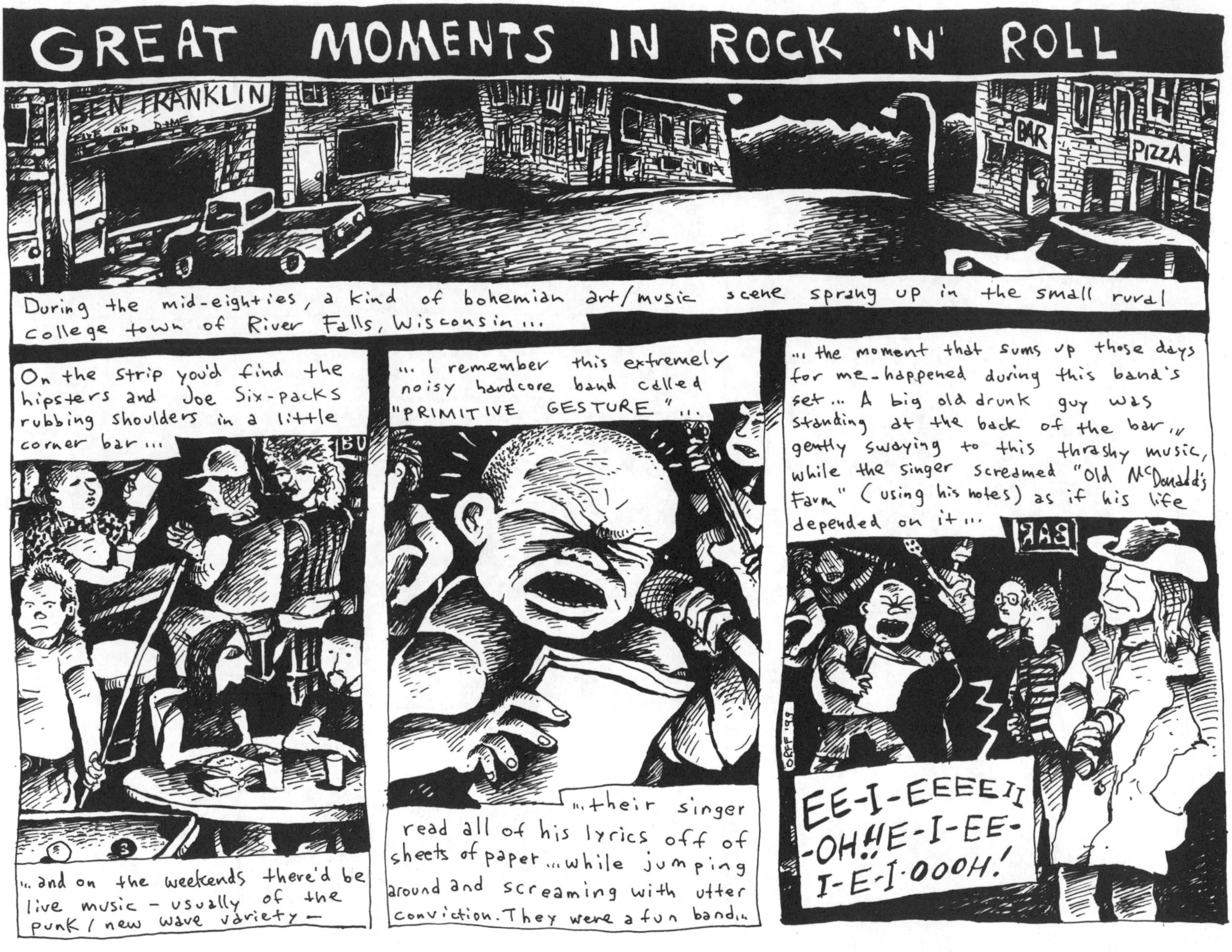
GREAT MOMENTS IN ROCK 'N' ROLL
BEN FRANKLIN
BAR
PIZZA
During the mid-eighties, a kind of bohemian art/music scene sprang up in the small rural college town of River Falls, Wisconsin...
On the strip you'd find the hipsters and Joe Six-packs rubbing shoulders in a little corner bar...
...and on the weekends there'd be live music - usually of the punk/new wave variety -
... I remember this extremely noisy hardcore band called "PRIMITIVE GESTURE"...
...their singer read all of his lyrics off of sheets of paper... while jumping around and screaming with utter conviction. They were a fun band...
... the moment that sums up those days for me - happened during this band's set... A big old drunk guy was standing at the back of the bar... gently swaying to this thrashy music, while the singer screamed "Old McDonald's Farm" (using his notes) as if his life depended on it...
EE-I-EEEEI! -OH!! E-I-EE- I-E-I-OOOH!

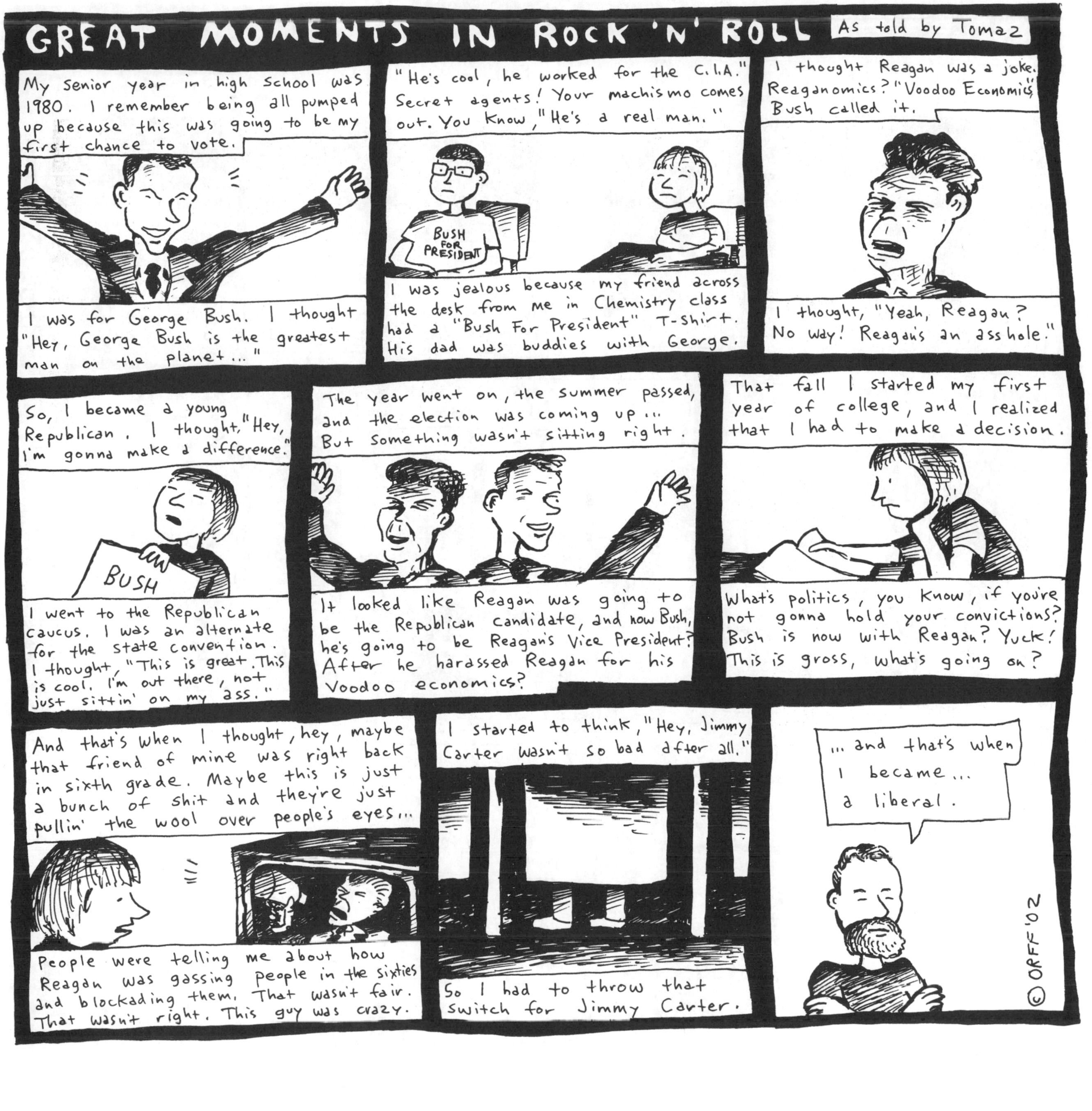
GREAT MOMENTS IN ROCK 'N' ROLL
As told by Tomaz
My senior year in high school was 1980. I remember being all pumped up because this was going to be my first chance to vote.
I was for George Bush. I thought "Hey, George Bush is the greatest man on the planet..."
"He's cool, he worked for the C.I.A." Secret agents! Your machismo comes out. You know, "He's a real man."
BUSH FOR PRESIDENT
I was jealous because my friend across the desk from me in Chemistry class had a "Bush For President" T-shirt. His dad was buddies with George.
I thought Reagan was a joke. Reaganomics? "Voodoo Economics" Bush called it.
I thought, "Yeah, Reagan? No way! Reagan's an asshole."
So, I became a young Republican. I thought, "Hey, I'm gonna make a difference."
BUSH
I went to the Republican caucus. I was an alternate for the state convention. I thought, "This is great. This is cool. I'm out there, not just sittin' on my ass."
The year went on, the summer passed, and the election was coming up... But something wasn't sitting right.
It looked like Reagan was going to be the Republican candidate, and now Bush, he's going to be Reagan's Vice President? After he harassed Reagan for his Voodoo economics?
That fall I started my first year of college, and I realized that I had to make a decision.
What's politics, you know, if you're not gonna hold your convictions? Bush is now with Reagan? Yuck! This is gross, what's going on?
And that's when I thought, hey, maybe that friend of mine was right back in sixth grade. Maybe this is just a bunch of shit and they're just pullin' the wool over people's eyes...
People were telling me about how Reagan was gassing people in the sixties and blockading them. That wasn't fair. That wasn't right. This guy was crazy.
I started to think, "Hey, Jimmy Carter wasn't so bad after all."
So I had to throw that switch for Jimmy Carter.
... and that's when I became... a liberal.
© ORFF '02

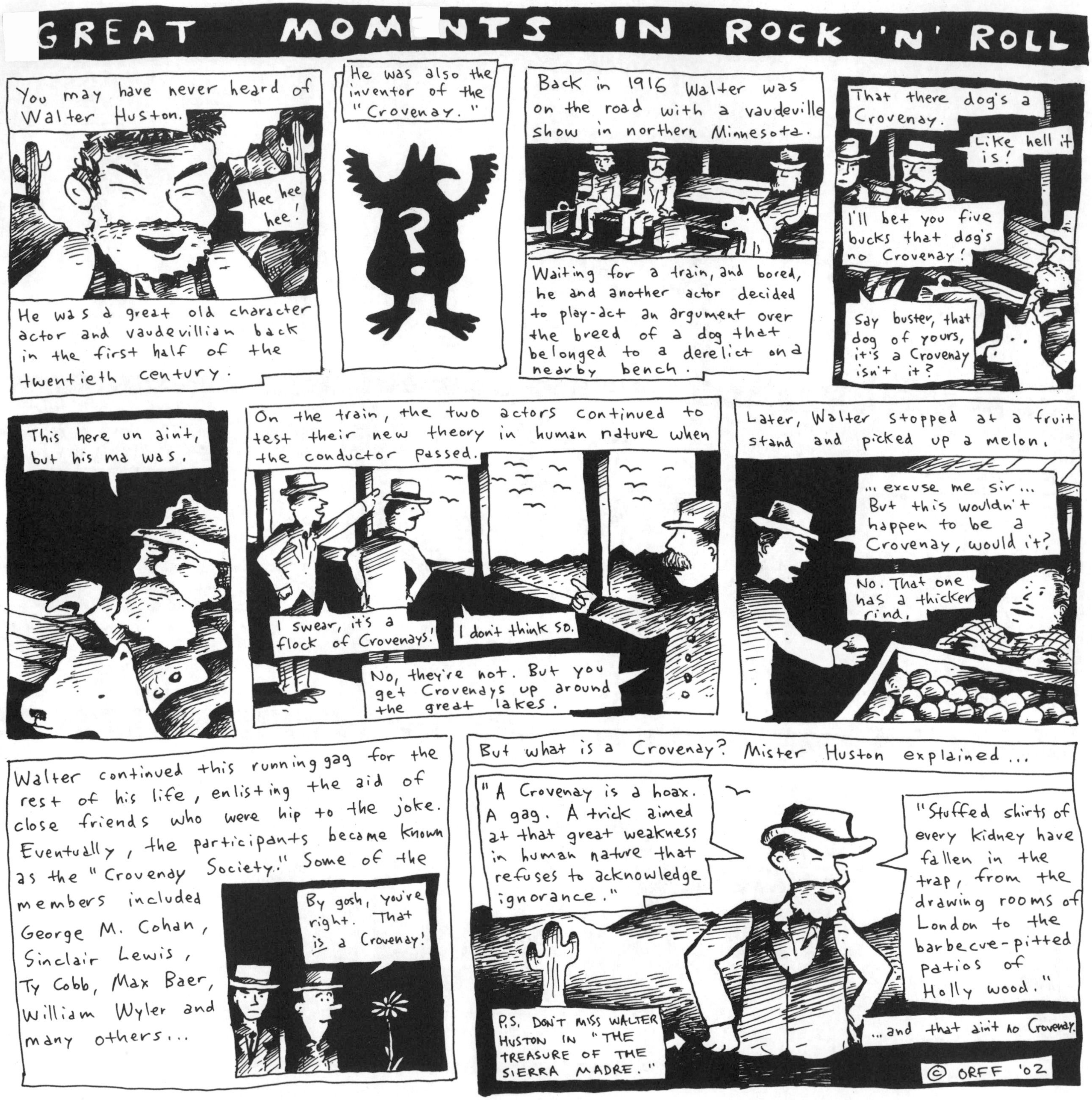
GREAT MOMENTS IN ROCK 'N' ROLL
You may have never heard of Walter Huston.
Hee hee hee!
He was a great old character actor and vaudevillian back in the first half of the twentieth century.
He was also the inventor of the "Crovenay."
?
Back in 1916 Walter was on the road with a vaudeville show in northern Minnesota.
Waiting for a train, and bored, he and another actor decided to play-act an argument over the breed of a dog that belonged to a derelict on a nearby bench.
That there dog's a Crovenay.
Like hell it is!
I'll bet you five bucks that dog's no Crovenay!
Say buster, that dog of yours, it's a Crovenay isn't it?
This here un aint, but his ma was.
On the train, the two actors continued to test their new theory in human nature when the conductor passed.
I swear, it's a flock of Crovenays!
I don't think so.
No, they're not. But you get Crovendys up around the great lakes.
Later, Walter stopped at a fruit stand and picked up a melon.
... excuse me sir... But this wouldn't happen to be a Crovenay, would it?
No. That one has a thicker rind.
Walter continued this running gag for the rest of his life, enlisting the aid of close friends who were hip to the joke. Eventually, the participants became known as the "Crovendy Society." Some of the members included George M. Cohan, Sinclair Lewis, Ty Cobb, Max Baer, William Wyler and many others...
By gosh, you're right. That is a Crovenay!
But what is a Crovenay? Mister Huston explained...
"A Crovenay is a hoax. A gag. A trick aimed at that great weakness in human nature that refuses to acknowledge ignorance."
"Stuffed shirts of every kidney have fallen in the trap, from the drawing rooms of London to the barbecue-pitted patios of Hollywood."
P.S. DON'T MISS WALTER HUSTON IN "THE TREASURE OF THE SIERRA MADRE."
...and that aint no Crovenay.
© ORFF '02

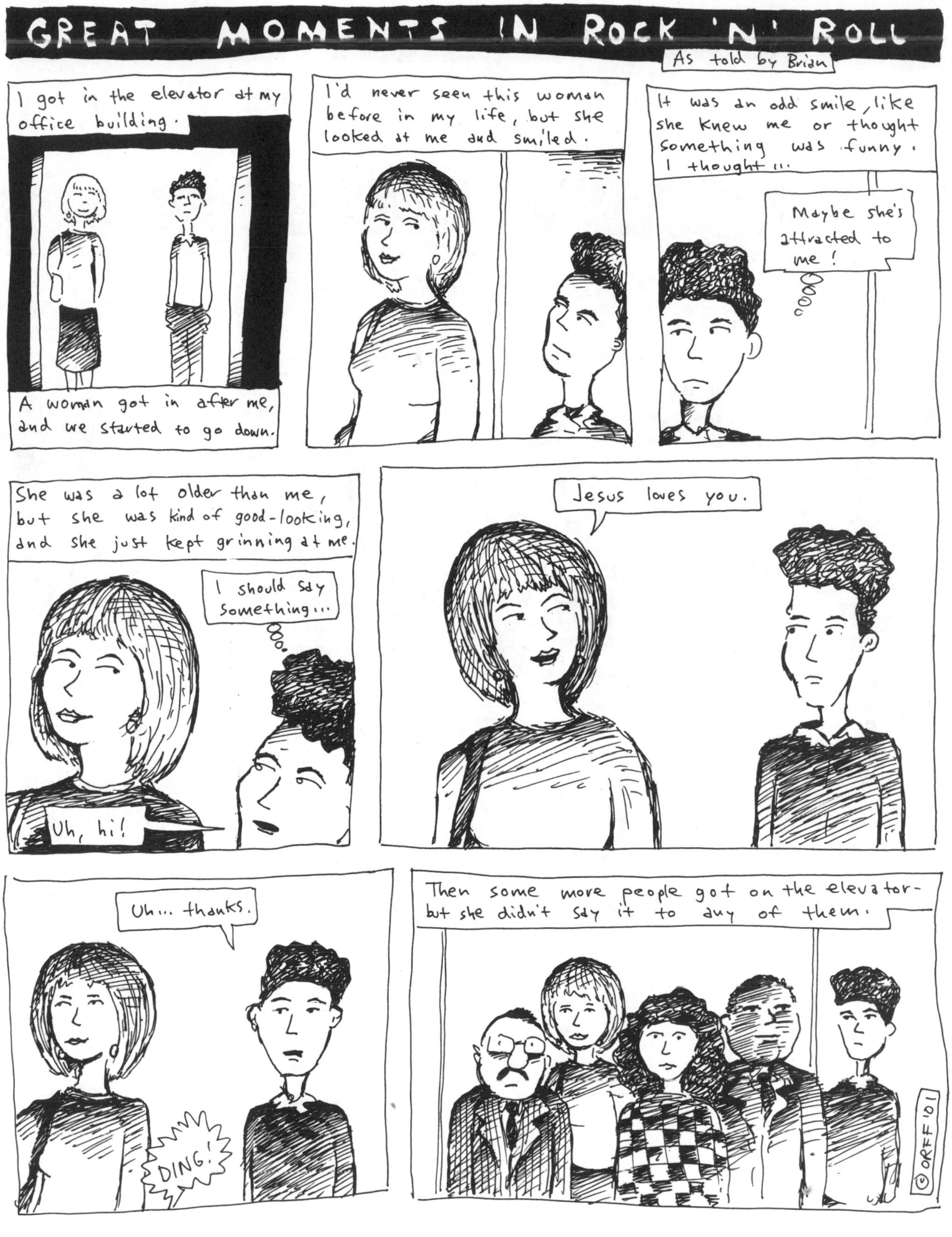
GREAT MOMENTS IN ROCK 'N' ROLL
As told by Brian
I got in the elevator at my office building.
A woman got in after me, and we started to go down.
I'd never seen this woman before in my life, but she looked at me and smiled.
It was an odd smile, like she knew me or thought something was funny. I thought...
Maybe she's attracted to me!
She was a lot older than me, but she was kind of good-looking, and she just kept grinning at me.
I should say something...
Uh, hi!
Jesus loves you.
Uh... thanks.
DING!
Then some more people got on the elevator- but she didn't say it to any of them.
©ORFF '01

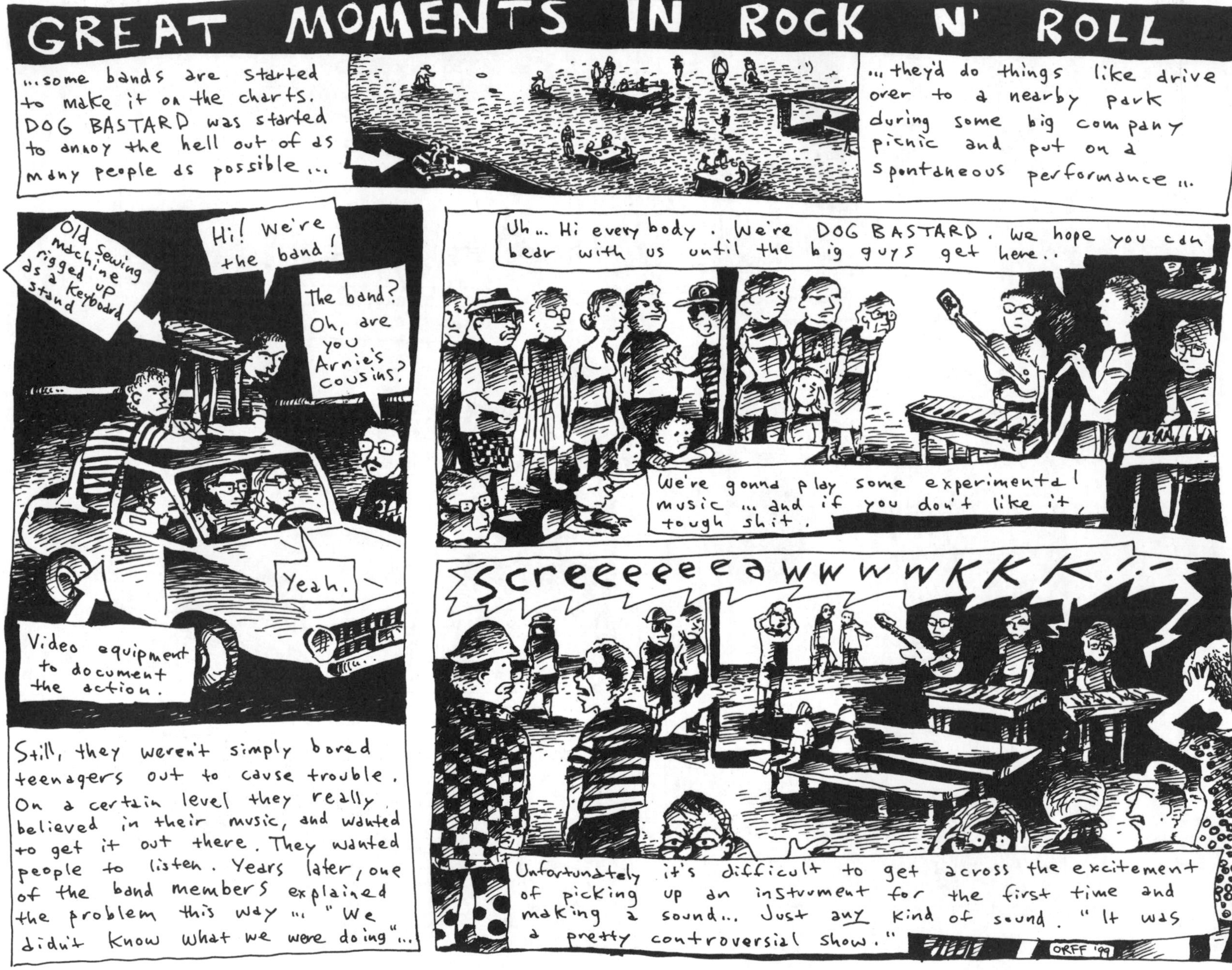
GREAT MOMENTS IN ROCK N' ROLL
...some bands are started to make it on the charts. DOG BASTARD was started to annoy the hell out of as many people as possible...
...they'd do things like drive over to a nearby park during some big company picnic and put on a spontaneous performance...
Old Sewing machine rigged up as a keyboard stand
Hi! We're the band!
The band? Oh, are you Arnie's cousins?
Yeah.
Video equipment to document the action.
Uh... Hi everybody. We're DOG BASTARD. We hope you can bear with us until the big guys get here..
We're gonna play some experimental music ... and if you don't like it, tough shit.
Still, they weren't simply bored teenagers out to cause trouble. On a certain level they really believed in their music, and wanted to get it out there. They wanted people to listen. Years later, one of the band members explained the problem this way... "We didn't know what we were doing"...
SCREEEEEEAWWWWKKK!!--
Unfortunately it's difficult to get across the excitement of picking up an instrument for the first time and making a sound... Just any kind of sound. "It was a pretty controversial show."
ORFF '99

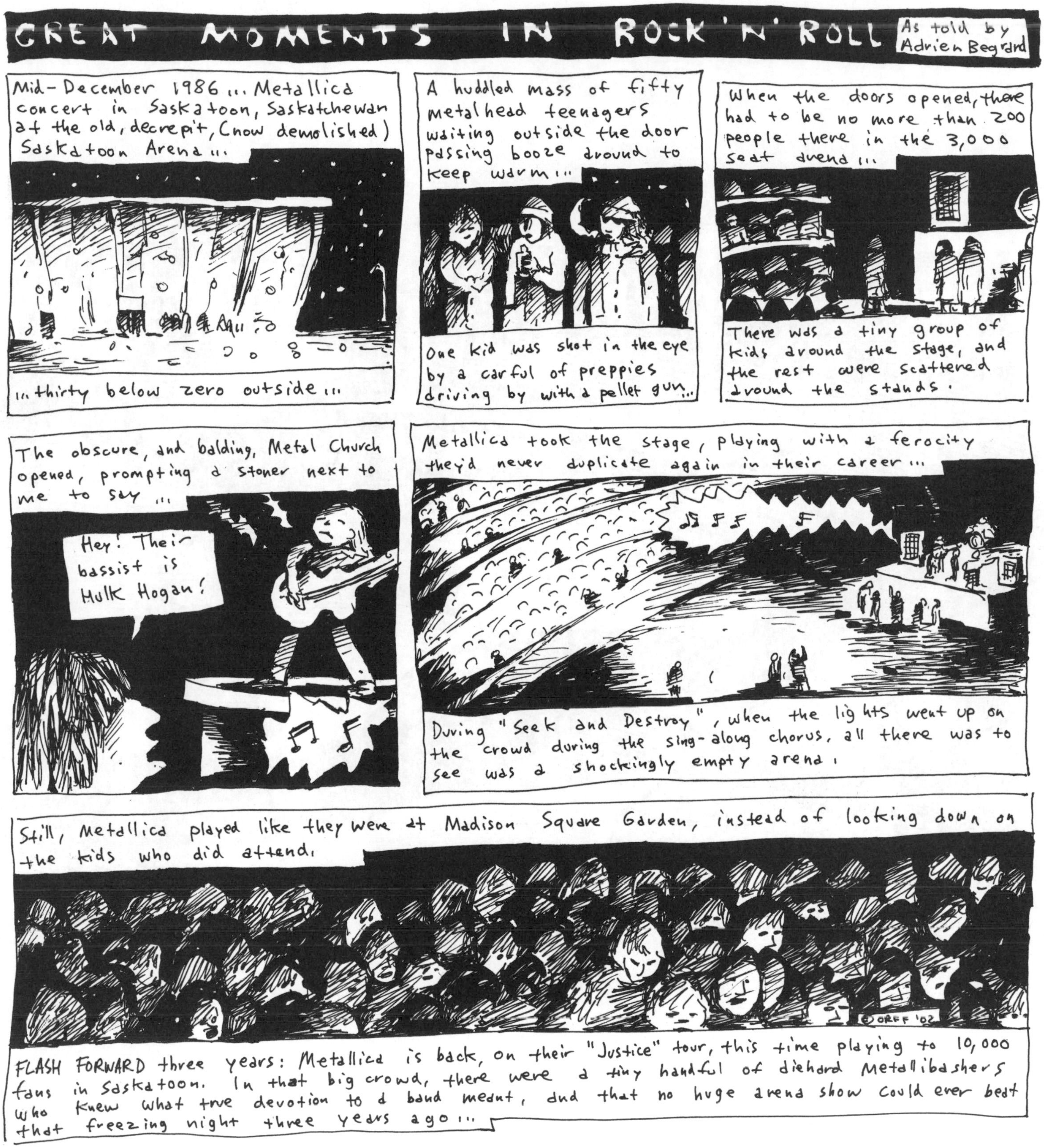
GREAT MOMENTS IN ROCK 'N' ROLL
As told by Adrien Begrand
Mid-December 1986... Metallica concert in Saskatoon, Saskatchewan at the old, decrepit, (now demolished) Saskatoon Arena...
...thirty below zero outside...
A huddled mass of fifty metalhead teenagers waiting outside the door passing booze around to keep warm...
One kid was shot in the eye by a carful of preppies driving by with a pellet gun...
When the doors opened, there had to be no more than 200 people there in the 3,000 seat arena...
There was a tiny group of kids around the stage, and the rest were scattered around the stands.
The obscure, and balding, Metal Church opened, prompting a stoner next to me to say...
Hey! Their bassist is Hulk Hogan!
Metallica took the stage, playing with a ferocity they'd never duplicate again in their career...
During "Seek and Destroy", when the lights went up on the crowd during the sing-along chorus, all there was to see was a shockingly empty arena.
Still, Metallica played like they were at Madison Square Garden, instead of looking down on the kids who did attend.
© ORFF '02
FLASH FORWARD three years: Metallica is back, on their "Justice" tour, this time playing to 10,000 fans in Saskatoon. In that big crowd, there were a tiny handful of diehard Metallibashers who knew what true devotion to a band meant, and that no huge arena show could ever beat that freezing night three years ago...

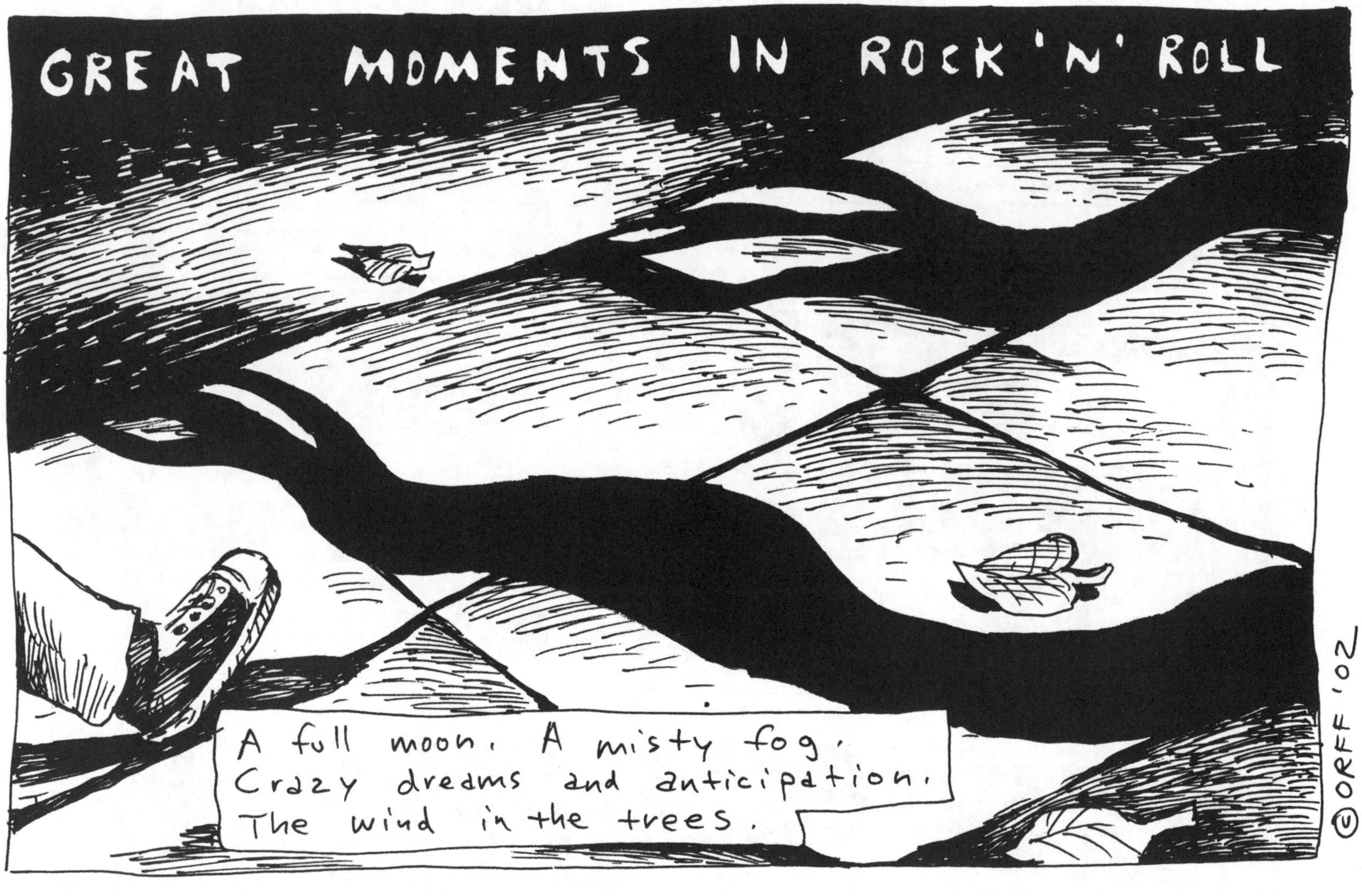
GREAT MOMENTS IN ROCK 'N' ROLL
A full moon. A misty fog.
Crazy dreams and anticipation.
The wind in the trees.
©ORFF '02

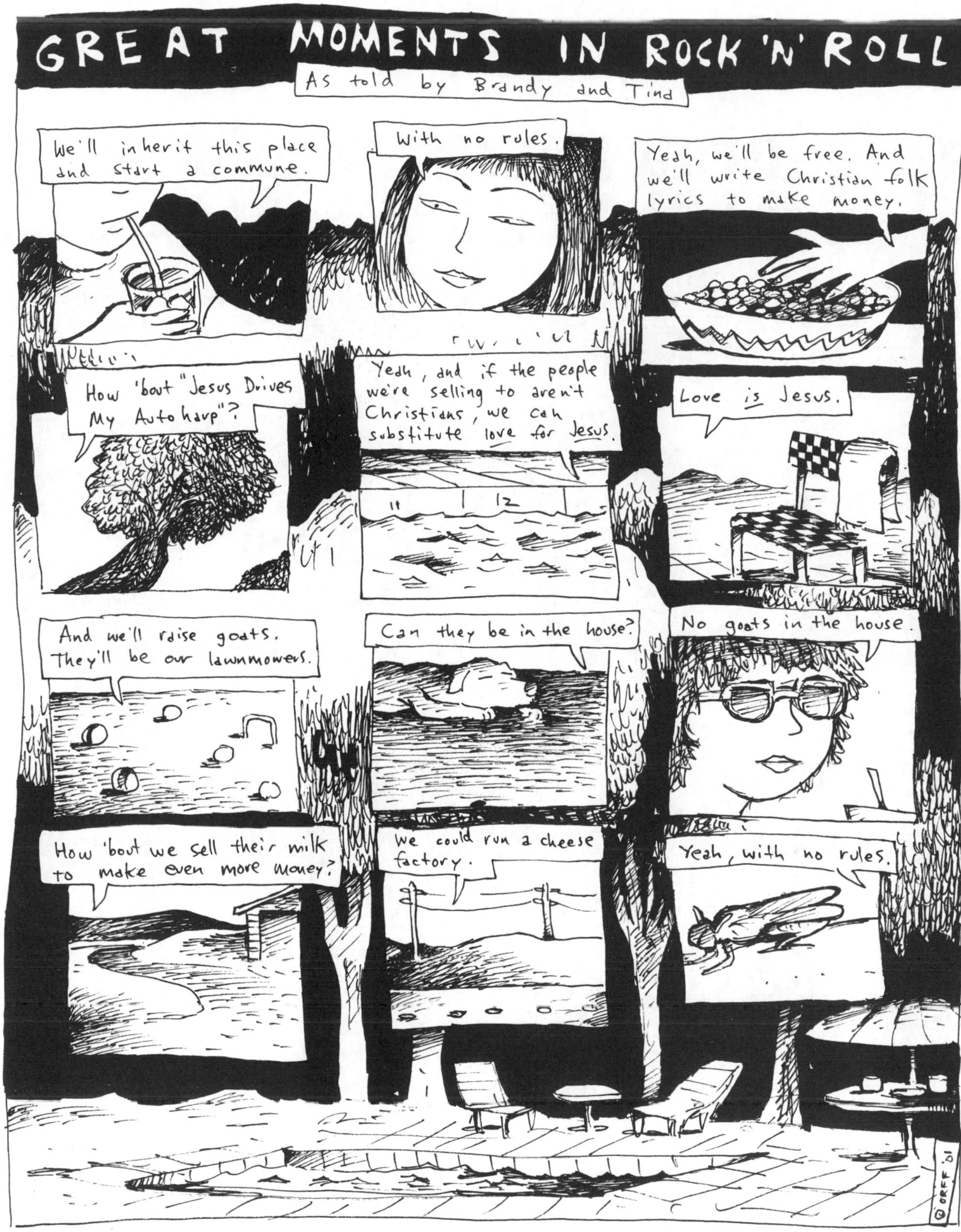
GREAT MOMENTS IN ROCK 'N' ROLL
As told by Brandy and Tina
We'll inherit this place and start a commune.
With no rules.
Yeah, we'll be free. And we'll write Christian folk lyrics to make money.
How 'bout "Jesus Drives My Autoharp"?
Yeah, and if the people we're selling to aren't Christians, we can substitute love for Jesus.
Love is Jesus.
And we'll raise goats. They'll be our lawnmowers.
Can they be in the house?
No goats in the house.
How 'bout we sell their milk to make even more money?
We could run a cheese factory.
Yeah, with no rules.
© ORFF '01

GREAT MOMENTS IN ROCK 'N' ROLL

As told by Nick Holz

"...we were already pretty drunk when we spotted it..."

"...A big old black wig..."

Somebody had just left it lying in the street.

It was really filthy, and we decided to add to it..."

Sticks, orange peels, cigarette butts... we stuck any shit we could find in there...

Then my buddy put it on and we got in line down at First Avenue for the MUDHONEY show.

All night he danced around, flinging his dirty "hair" in everyone's face...

"...near the end of the show he threw the wig onto the stage...

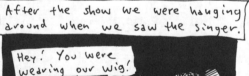

When the band came back for their encore... the lead singer was wearing our stinky old wig!

He was doing some fake rock star prancing around... having fun with it... orange peels were flying...

After the show we were hanging around when we saw the singer.

Hey! You were wearing our wig!

Hey man... you know, we found that thing in the gutter...

...really?

Uhhhg.... what if there was poop in it?

60

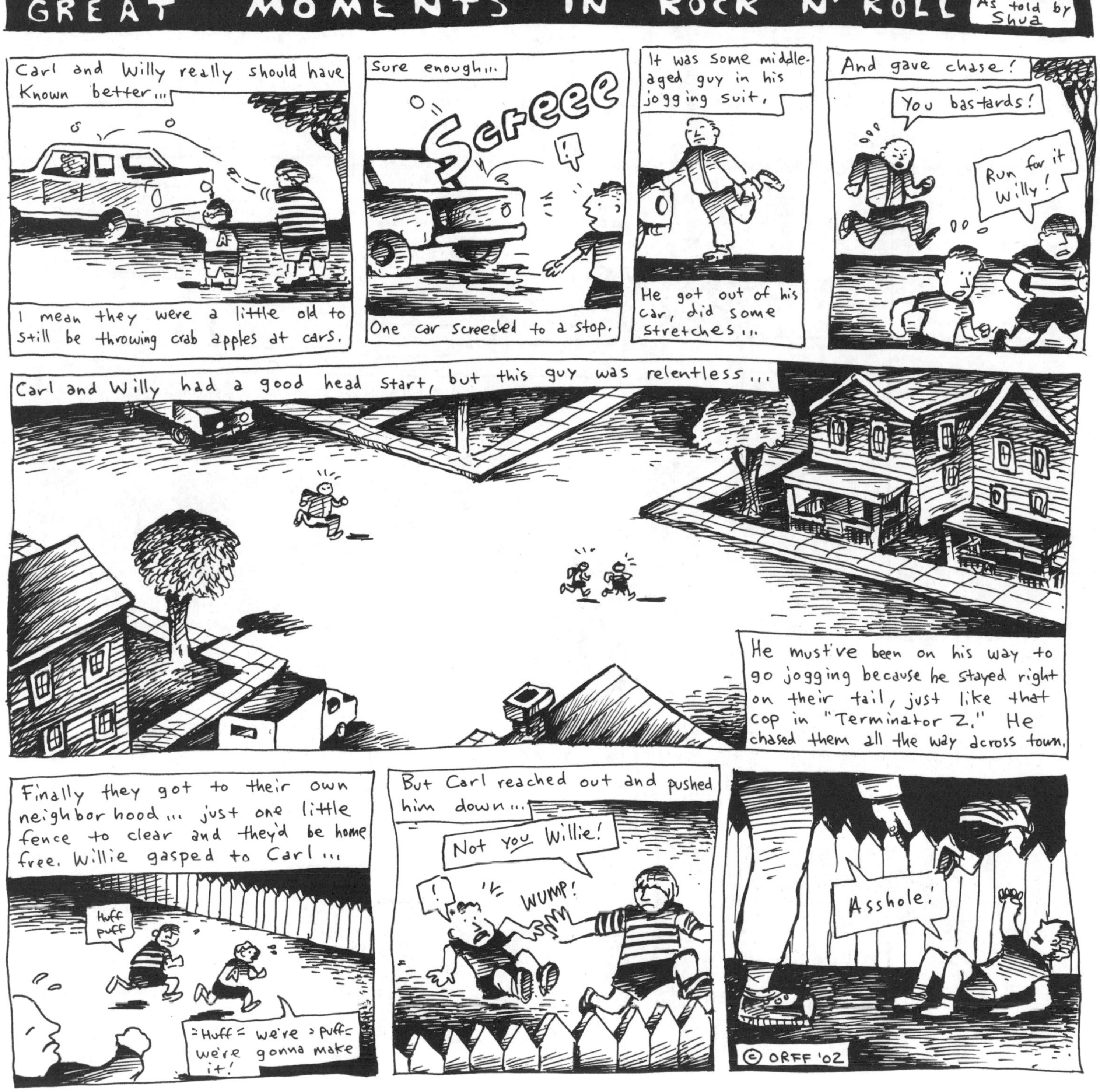
GREAT MOMENTS IN ROCK 'N' ROLL
As told by Shua
Carl and Willy really should have Known better...
I mean they were a little old to still be throwing crab apples at cars.
Sure enough...
Screee
!
One car screeched to a stop.
It was some middle-aged guy in his jogging suit,
He got out of his car, did some stretches...
And gave chase!
You bastards!
Run for it Willy!
Carl and Willy had a good head start, but this guy was relentless...
He must've been on his way to go jogging because he stayed right on their tail, just like that cop in "Terminator 2." He chased them all the way across town.
Finally they got to their own neighborhood... just one little fence to clear and they'd be home free. Willie gasped to Carl...
Huff puff
=Huff= we're =puff= we're gonna make it!
But Carl reached out and pushed him down...
Not you Willie!
!
WUMP!
Asshole!
© ORFF '02

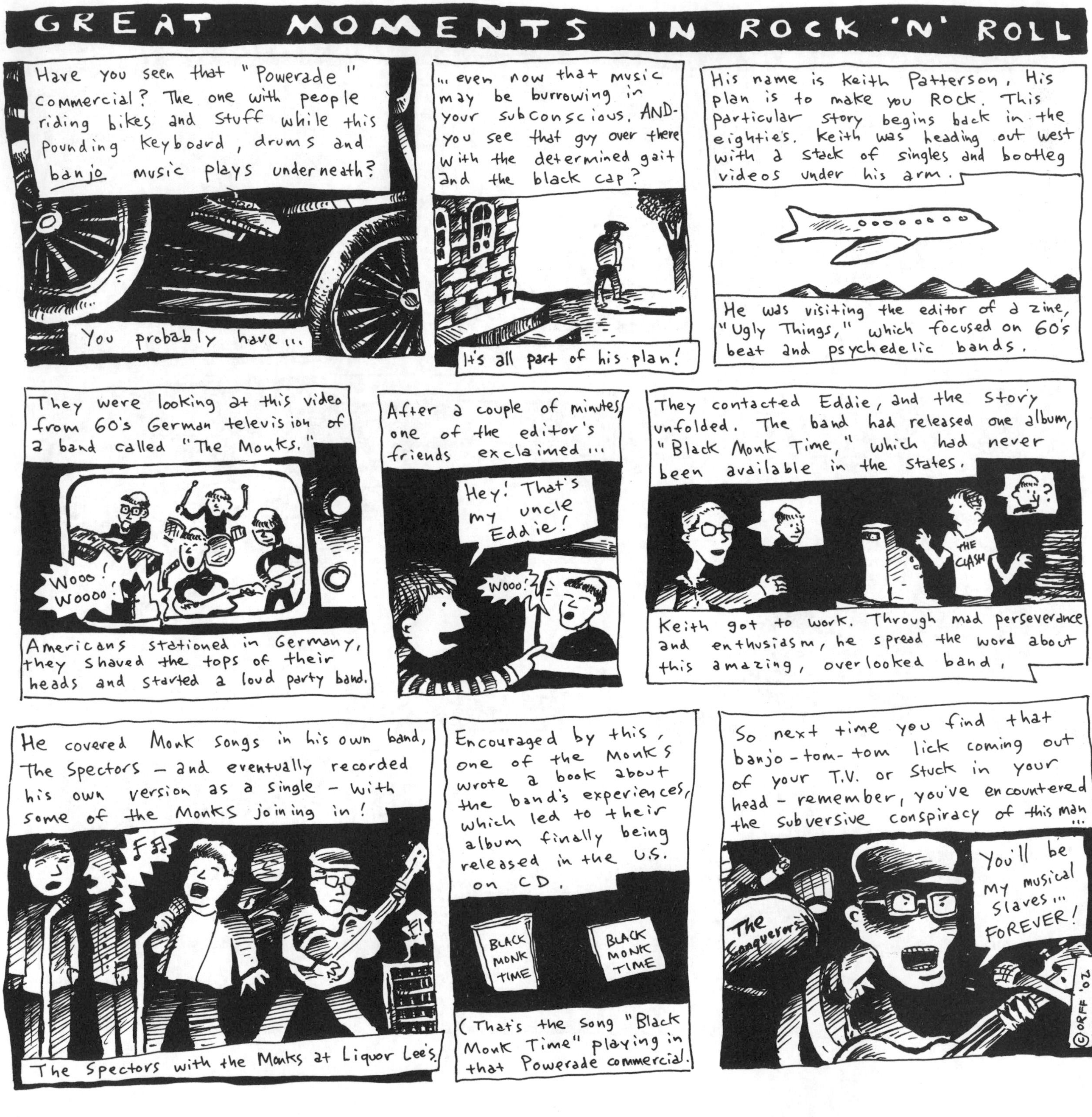
GREAT MOMENTS IN ROCK 'N' ROLL
Have you seen that "Powerade" commercial? The one with people riding bikes and stuff while this pounding keyboard, drums and banjo music plays underneath?
You probably have...
...even now that music may be burrowing in your subconscious. AND- you see that guy over there with the determined gait and the black cap?
It's all part of his plan!
His name is Keith Patterson. His plan is to make you ROCK. This particular story begins back in the eighties. Keith was heading out west with a stack of singles and bootleg videos under his arm.
He was visiting the editor of a zine, "Ugly Things," which focused on 60's beat and psychedelic bands.
They were looking at this video from 60's German television of a band called "The Monks."
Wooo! Woooo!
Americans stationed in Germany, they shaved the tops of their heads and started a loud party band.
After a couple of minutes, one of the editor's friends exclaimed...
Hey! That's my uncle Eddie!
Wooo!
They contacted Eddie, and the story unfolded. The band had released one album, "Black Monk Time," which had never been available in the States.
THE CLASH
?
Keith got to work. Through mad perseverance and enthusiasm, he spread the word about this amazing, overlooked band.
He covered Monk songs in his own band, The Spectors - and eventually recorded his own version as a single - with some of the Monks joining in!
The Spectors with the Monks at Liquor Lee's.
Encouraged by this, one of the Monks wrote a book about the band's experiences, which led to their album finally being released in the U.S. on CD.
BLACK MONK TIME
BLACK MONK TIME
(That's the song "Black Monk Time" playing in that Powerade commercial.)
So next time you find that banjo-tom-tom lick coming out of your T.V. or stuck in your head - remember, you've encountered the subversive conspiracy of this man...
You'll be my musical slaves... FOREVER!
The Conquerors
© ORFF '02

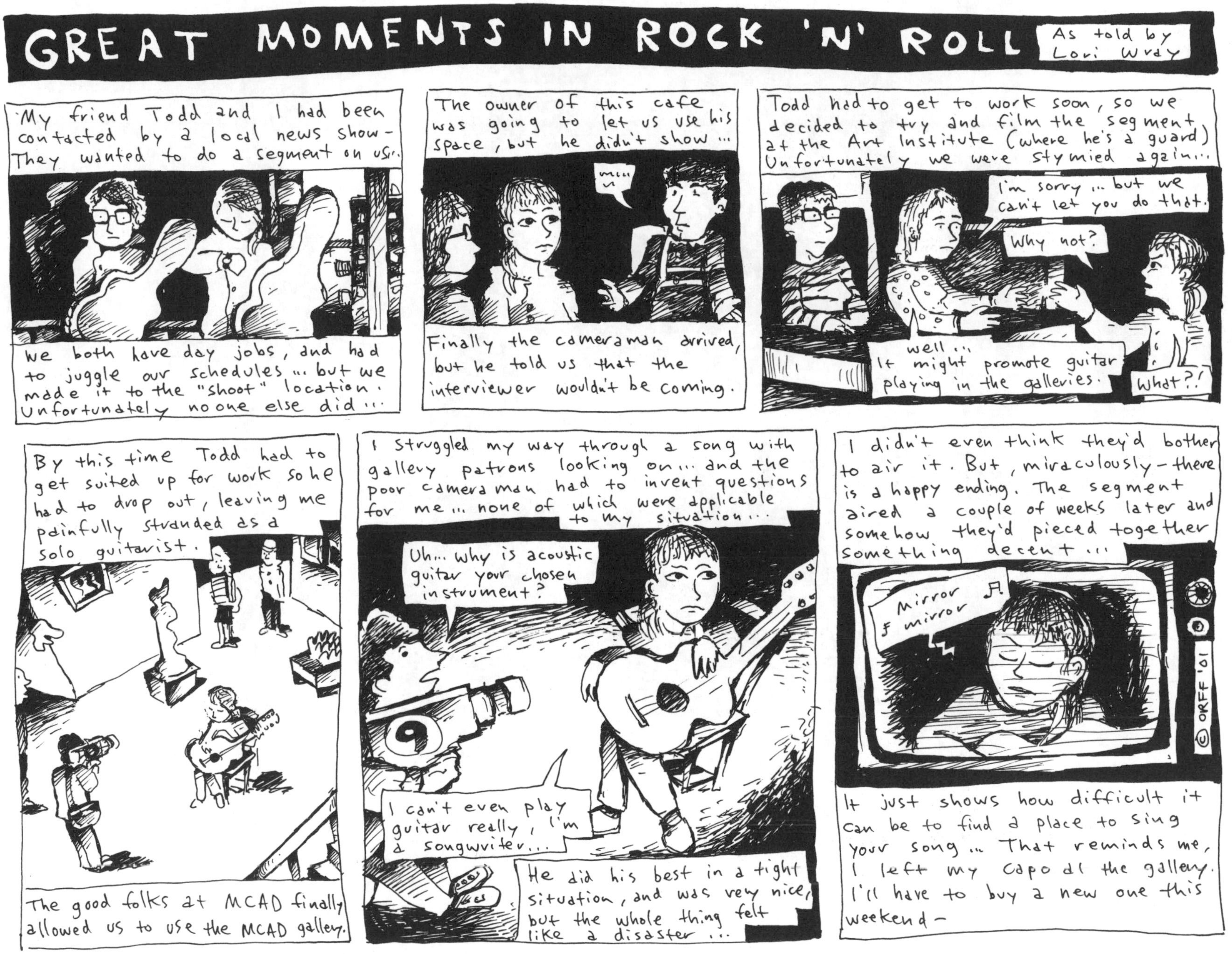
GREAT MOMENTS IN ROCK 'N' ROLL
As told by Lori Wray
My friend Todd and I had been contacted by a local news show - They wanted to do a segment on us...
We both have day jobs, and had to juggle our schedules... but we made it to the "shoot" location. Unfortunately no one else did...
The owner of this cafe was going to let us use his space, but he didn't show...
mm... u
Finally the cameraman arrived, but he told us that the interviewer wouldn't be coming.
Todd had to get to work soon, so we decided to try and film the segment at the Art Institute (where he's a guard) Unfortunately we were stymied again...
I'm sorry... but we can't let you do that.
Why not?
well... It might promote guitar playing in the galleries.
What?!
By this time Todd had to get suited up for work so he had to drop out, leaving me painfully stranded as a solo guitarist.
The good folks at MCAD finally allowed us to use the MCAD gallery.
I struggled my way through a song with gallery patrons looking on... and the poor cameraman had to invent questions for me... none of which were applicable to my situation...
Uh... why is acoustic guitar your chosen instrument?
I can't even play guitar really, I'm a songwriter...
He did his best in a tight situation, and was very nice, but the whole thing felt like a disaster...
I didn't even think they'd bother to air it. But, miraculously - there is a happy ending. The segment aired a couple of weeks later and somehow they'd pieced together something decent...
Mirror mirror
© ORFF '01
It just shows how difficult it can be to find a place to sing your song... That reminds me, I left my capo at the gallery. I'll have to buy a new one this weekend -

tattoo

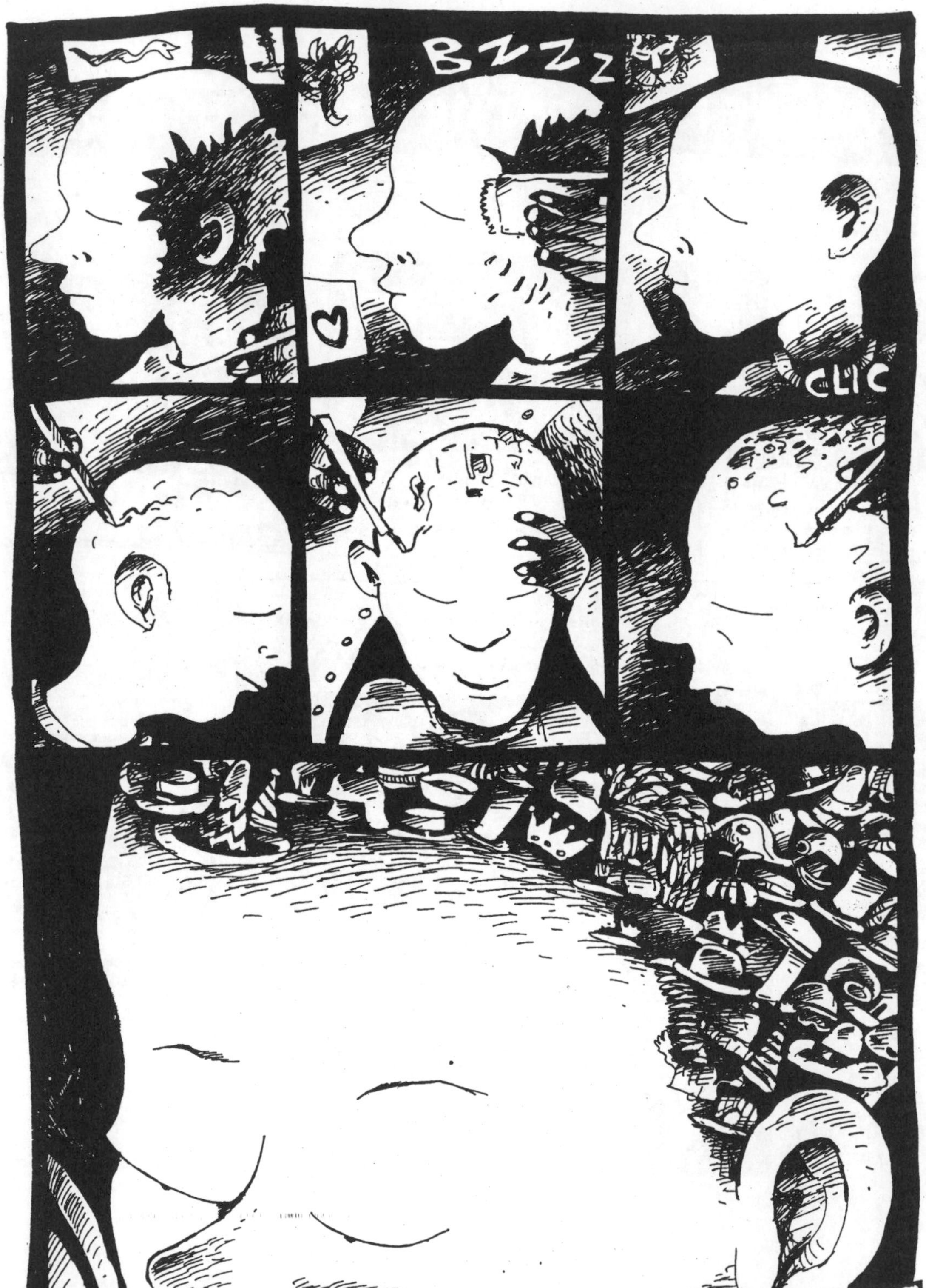
BZZZZ
CLIC
ORFF! '02

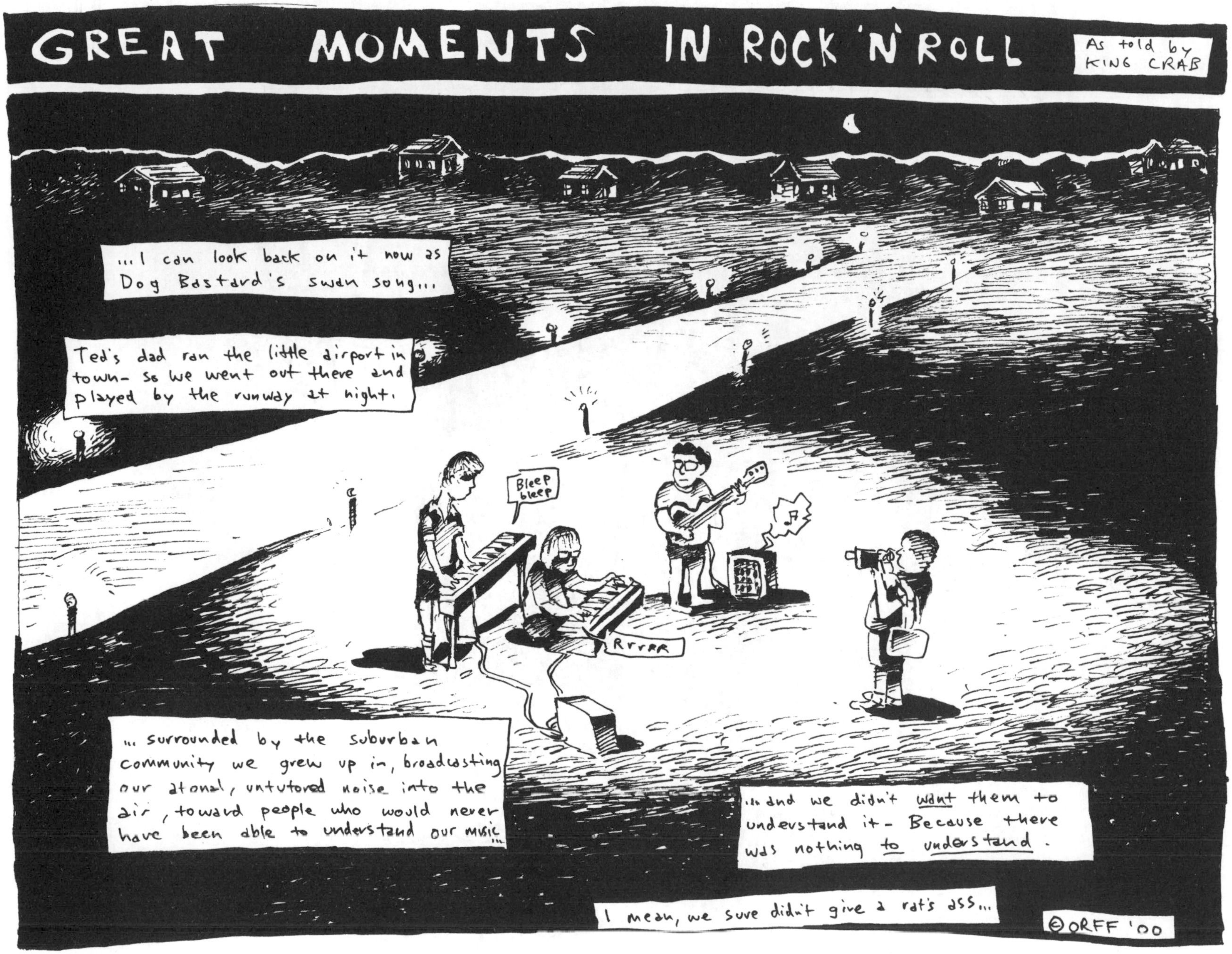
GREAT MOMENTS IN ROCK 'N' ROLL
As told by KING CRAB
...I can look back on it now as Dog Bastard's swan song...
Ted's dad ran the little airport in town- so we went out there and played by the runway at night.
Bleep bleep
Rrrrr
... surrounded by the suburban community we grew up in, broadcasting our atonal, untutored noise into the air, toward people who would never have been able to understand our music...
...and we didn't want them to understand it- Because there was nothing to understand.
I mean, we sure didn't give a rat's ass...
©ORFF '00

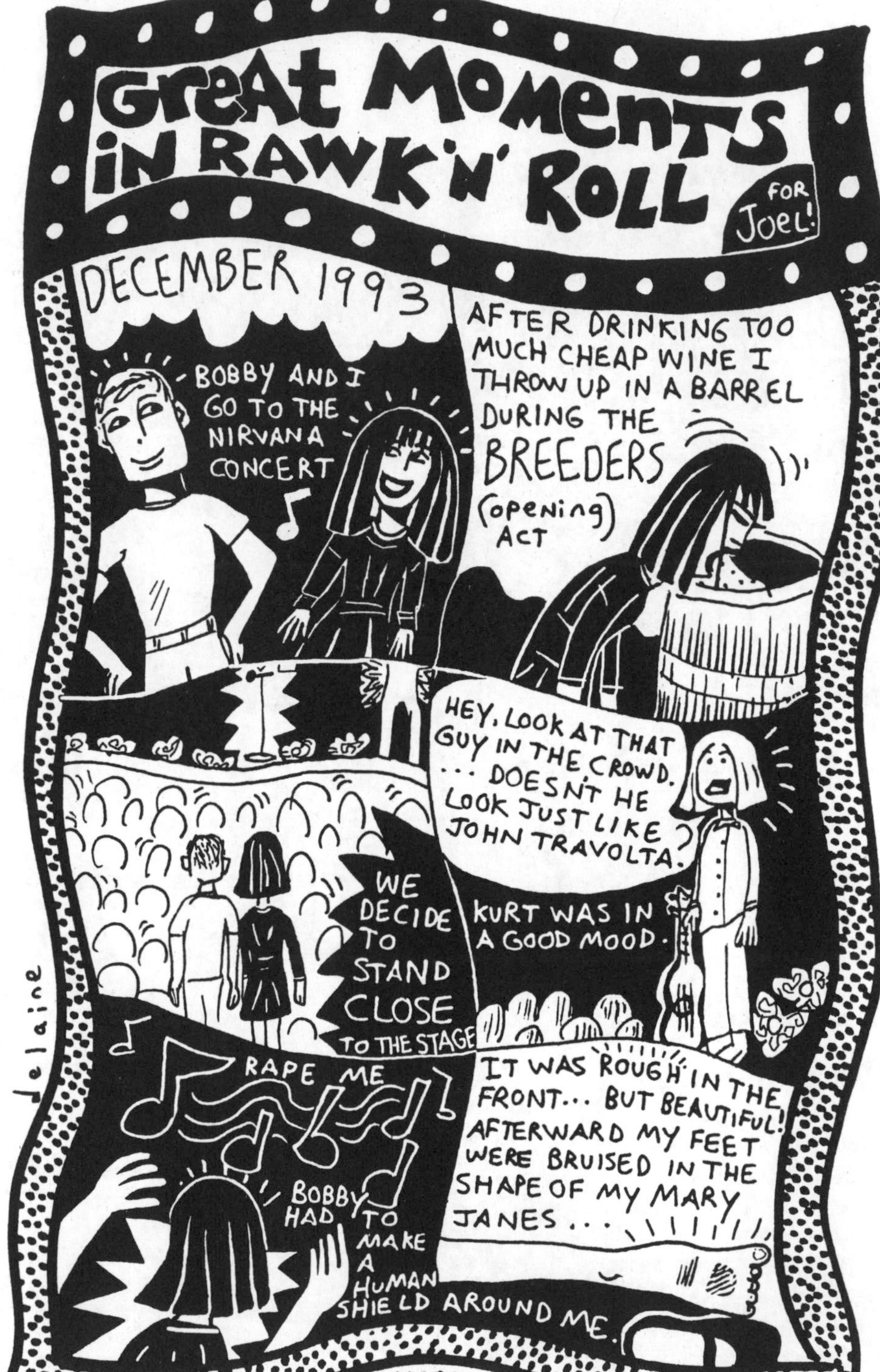
GREAT MOMENTS IN RAWK 'N' ROLL
FOR JOEL!
DECEMBER 1993
BOBBY AND I GO TO THE NIRVANA CONCERT
AFTER DRINKING TOO MUCH CHEAP WINE I THROW UP IN A BARREL DURING THE BREEDERS (opening) ACT
HEY, LOOK AT THAT GUY IN THE CROWD... DOESN'T HE LOOK JUST LIKE JOHN TRAVOLTA?
WE DECIDE TO STAND CLOSE TO THE STAGE
KURT WAS IN A GOOD MOOD.
RAPE ME
IT WAS ROUGH IN THE FRONT... BUT BEAUTIFUL! AFTERWARD MY FEET WERE BRUISED IN THE SHAPE OF MY MARY JANES...
BOBBY HAD TO MAKE A HUMAN SHIELD AROUND ME.
MY FAVORITE SHOW.
Delaine

I drew this in honor of Joel Orff and HIS *Great Moments in Rock 'n' Roll*

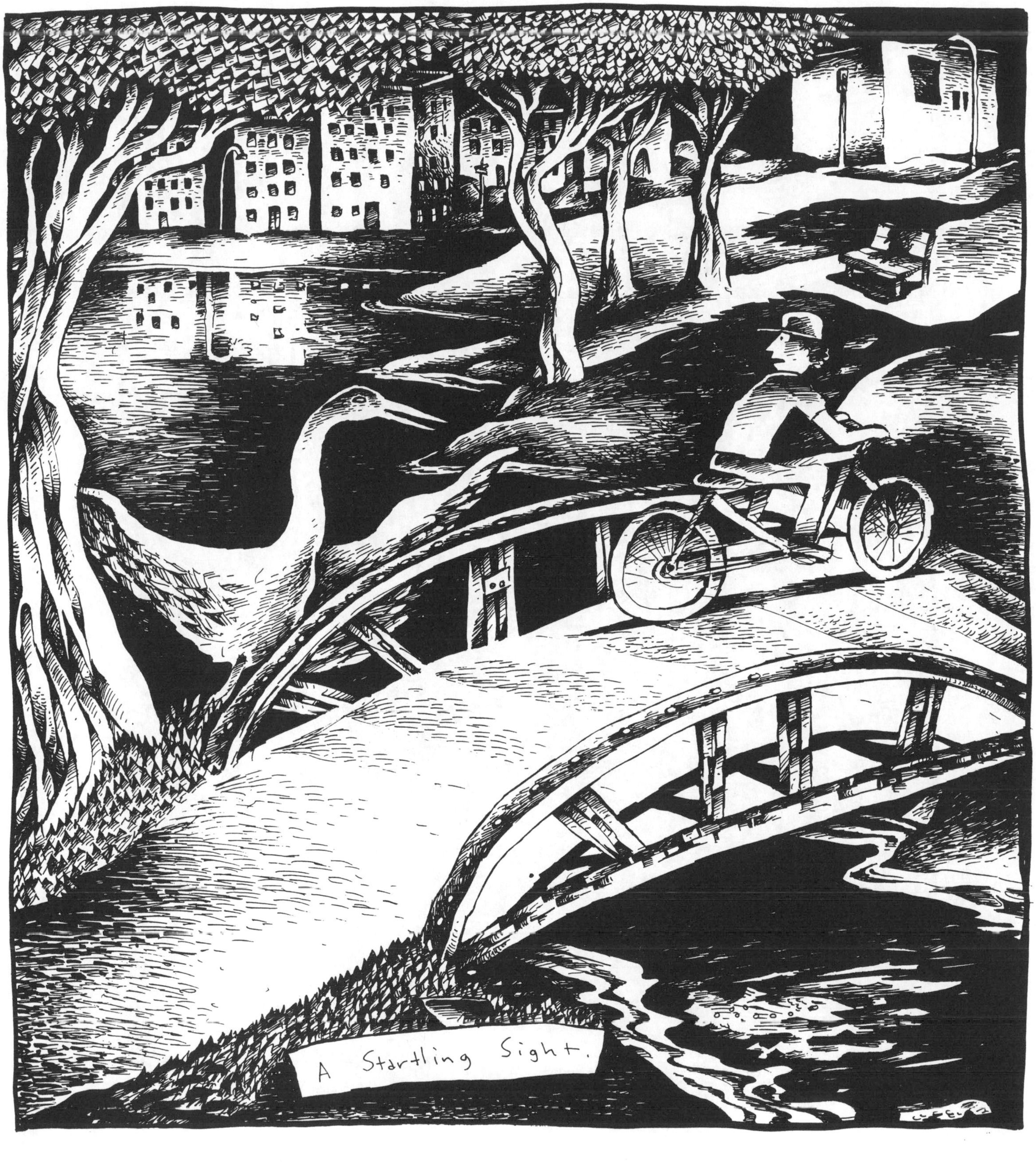
A Startling Sight.

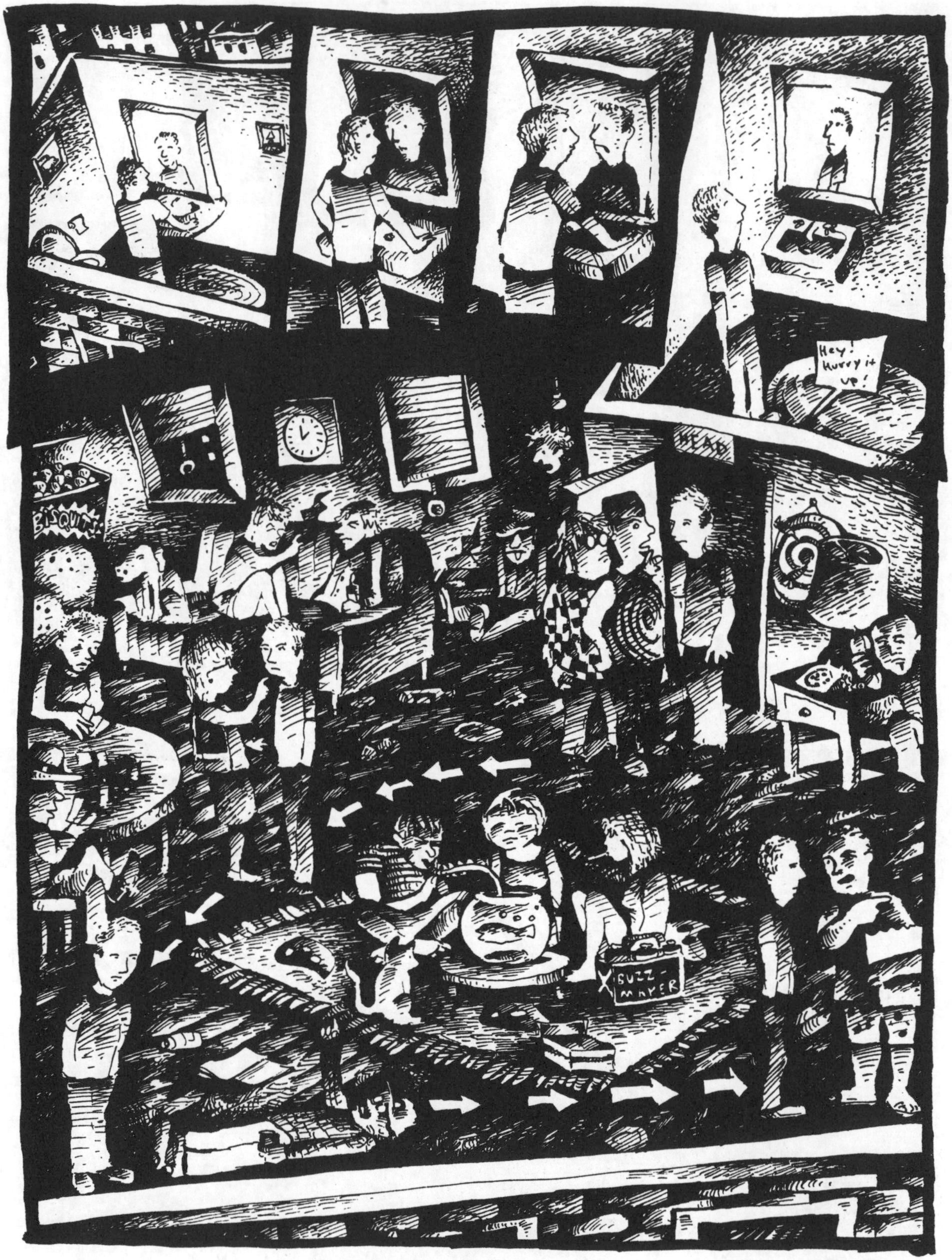
Hey! Hurry it up!
HEAD
BISQUITS
BUZZ-MAKER

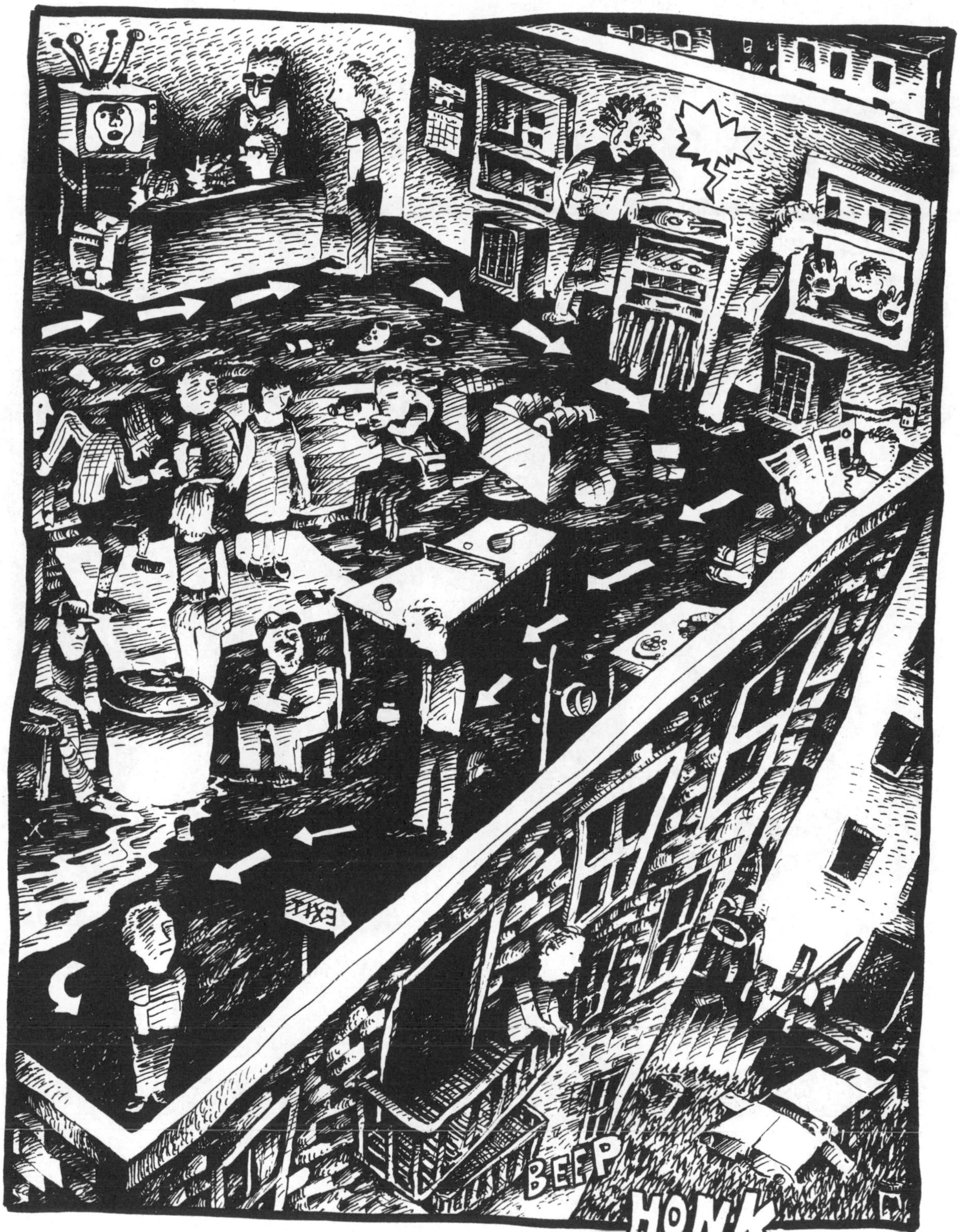
EXIT
BEEP
HONK

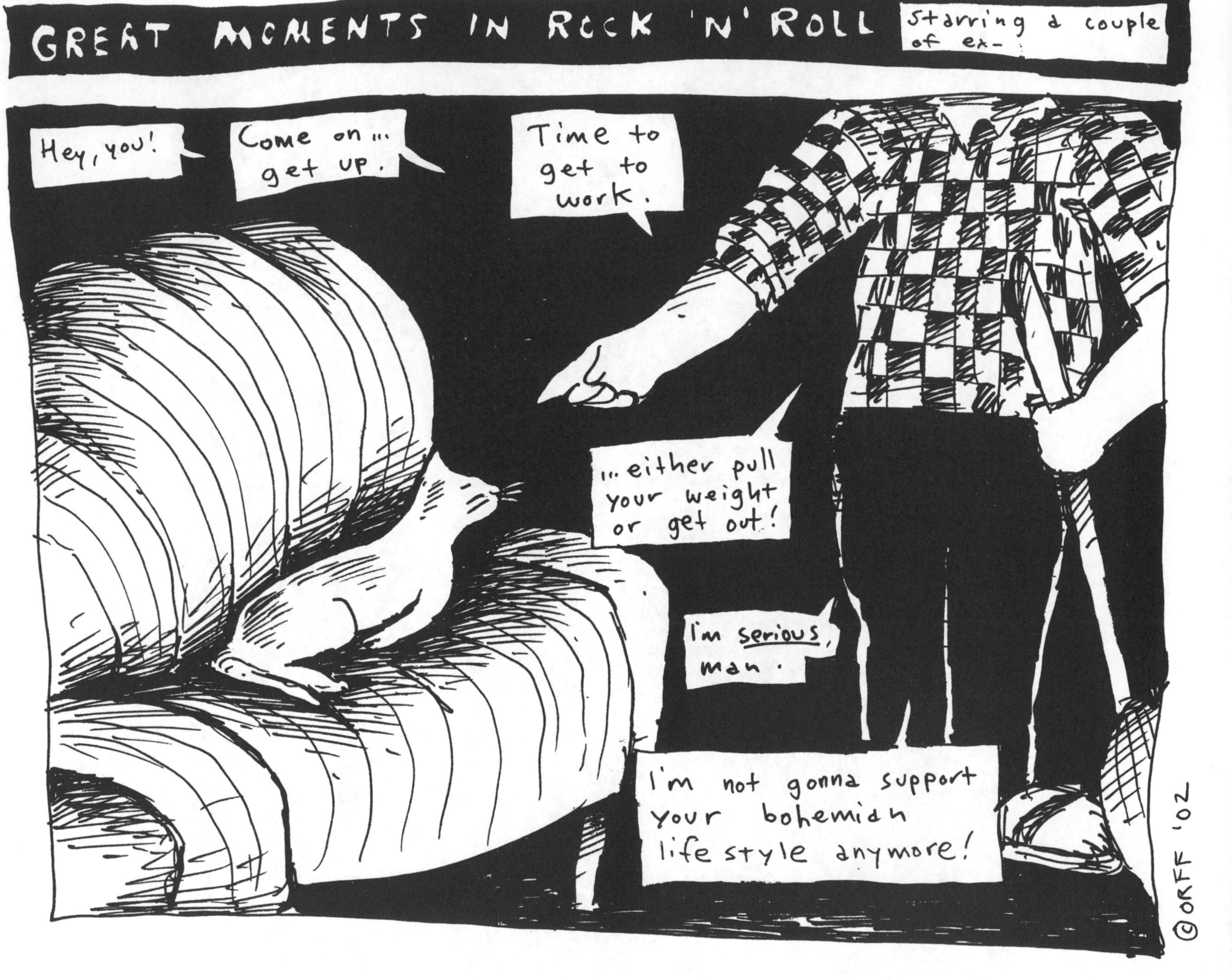
GREAT MOMENTS IN ROCK 'N' ROLL
Starring a couple of ex-
Hey, you!
Come on... get up.
Time to get to work.
...either pull your weight or get out!
I'm serious, man.
I'm not gonna support your bohemian lifestyle anymore!
©ORFF '02

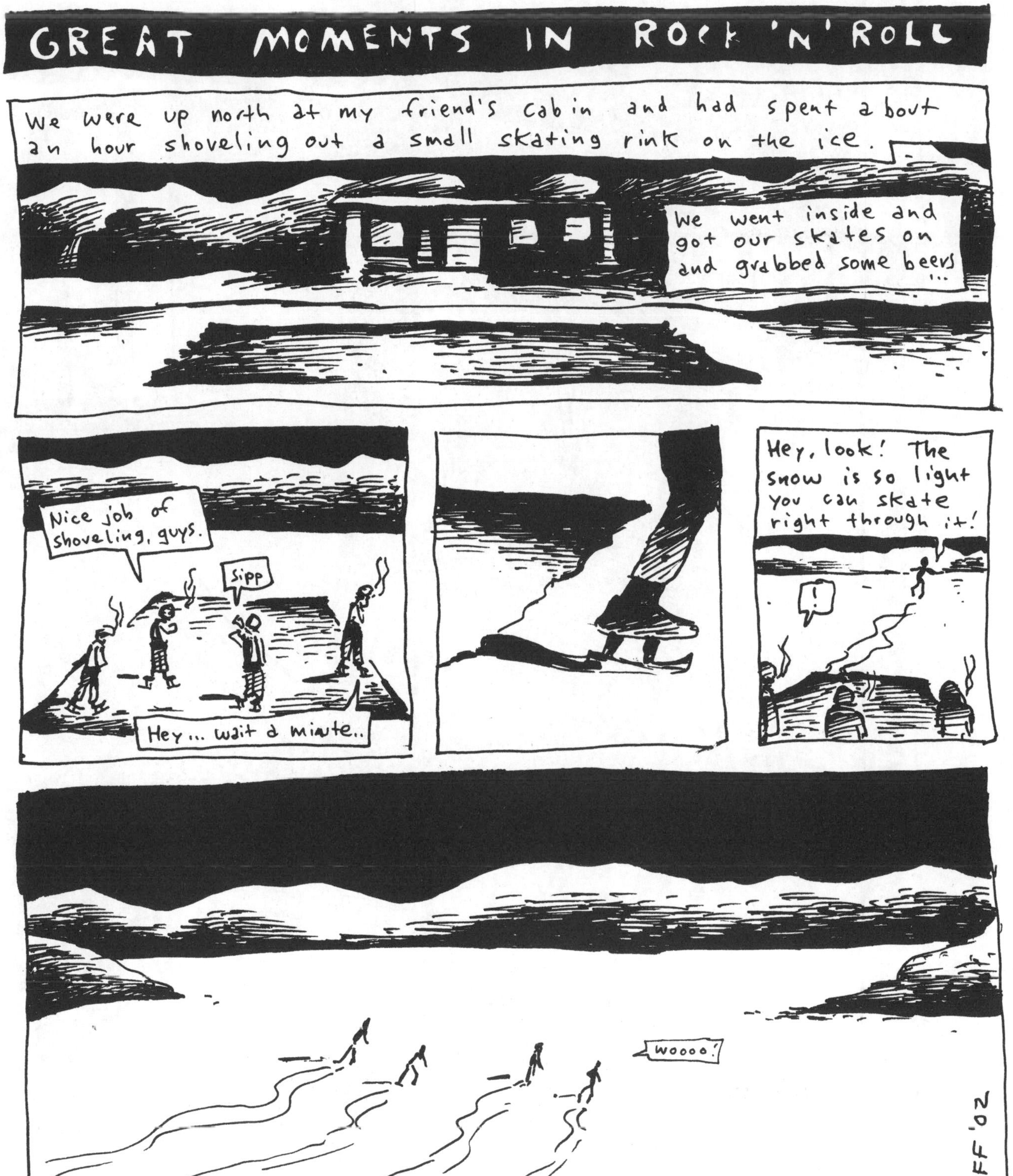
GREAT MOMENTS IN ROCK 'N' ROLL
We were up north at my friend's cabin and had spent about an hour shoveling out a small skating rink on the ice.
We went inside and got our skates on and grabbed some beers...
Nice job of shoveling, guys.
Sipp
Hey... wait a minute..
Hey, look! The snow is so light you can skate right through it!
!
Woooo!
© ORFF '02

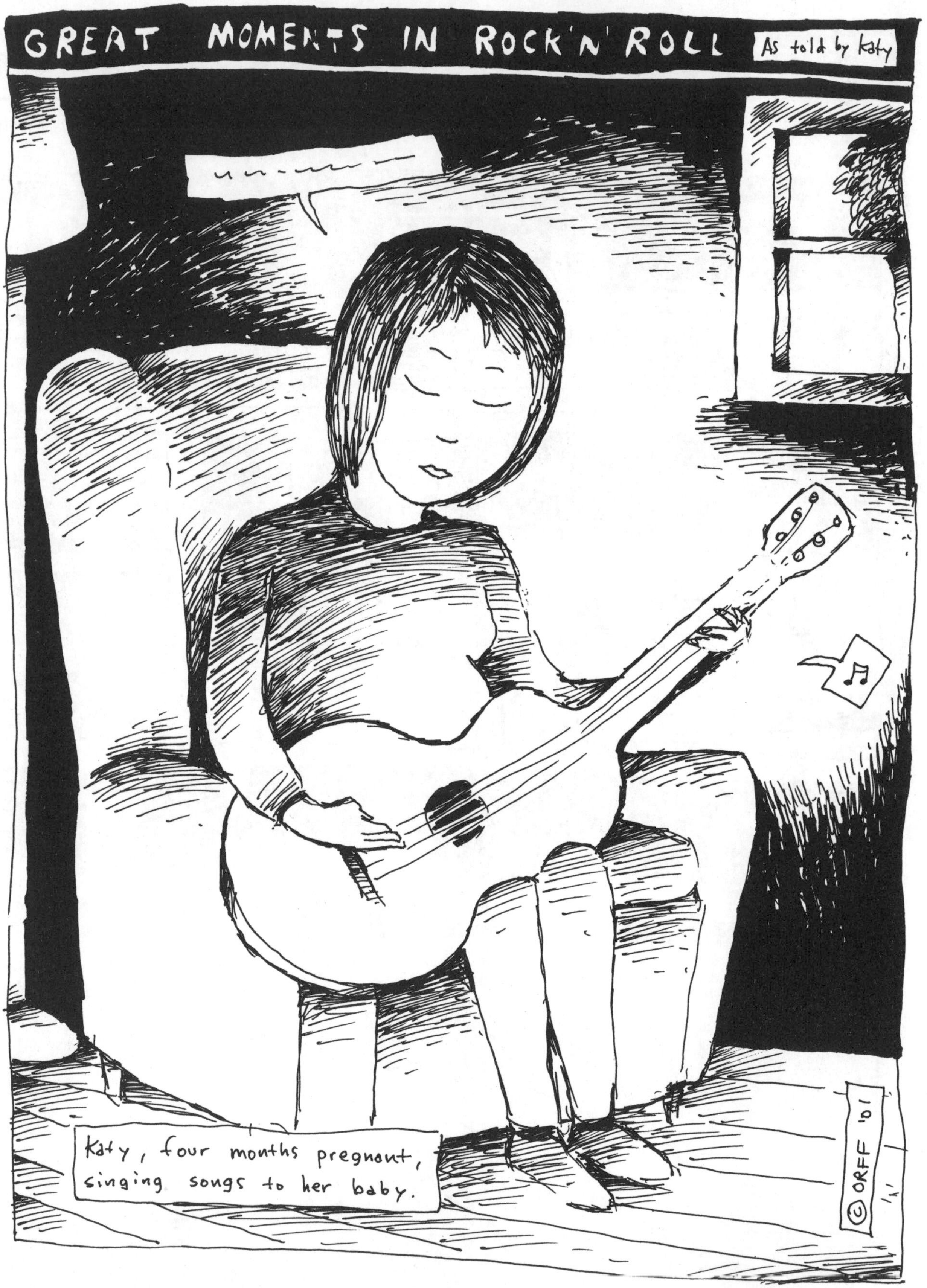
GREAT MOMENTS IN ROCK 'N' ROLL
As told by katy
Katy, four months pregnant, singing songs to her baby.
© ORFF '01